QUINTON HAZELL

The Life of an Entrepreneur

QUINTON HAZELL

The Life of an Entrepreneur

Quinton Hazell

ALAN SUTTON

First published in the United Kingdom in 1992
Alan Sutton Publishing Ltd · Phoenix Mill · Far Thrupp · Stroud
Gloucestershire

British Library Cataloguing in Publication Data

Hazell, Quinton
Quinton Hazell: The Life of an Entrepreneur
I. Title
338.7

ISBN 0-7509-0246-9

Typesetting and origination by
Alan Sutton Publishing Limited.
Printed in Great Britain.

CONTENTS

ILLUSTRATIONS

PREFACE

This short story chronicles events in my life which I thought a
reader might find of interest.

I write of my early life, because I had such a happy childhood
and the Garden Village, Burnage, Manchester was rather special for
those of us who grew up there. I describe my childhood after the
Great War and comment on the atmosphere in those immediate
post war years: the tragedies of the returned soldiers, the gentleness
of those who returned, and their care and devotion to their children. It was a trusting world: burglaries were almost unheard of and
murder made headline news for a fortnight. My uncle's house in
Barnham Broom, Norfolk, did not even have a front door key.

Mothers by and large stayed at home, and fathers were the bread-
winners. School was disciplined but fair. Honouring Great Britain
and the Union Flag was an important part of our education. There
was no television of course, and the crystal wireless set with head-
phones was the only recreation we did not make ourselves. At
home, Aunt Dolly played the piano, Father the fiddle and Uncle
Harry sang. At the local cinema, the motion pictures were silent
and a piano or organ in the pit provided the mood music.

You will readily see that in this environment we had to make our
own pastimes. From an early age, sports of all types were our main
pleasures. This regime in early life helped us as children to appreciate discipline and respect our teachers, and above all to appreciate
the country in which we were born, and our heritage. We were
taught to work together as a team and always to try to help each
other. Thus my early life progressed.

As I grew older, working in my father's workshop became a
major interest. He taught me to appreciate wood, how to shape it,
glue and join. Father taught me to use chisels and saws, and I soon

appreciated that when using a lathe, drill or other machinery, I had to concentrate on the job in hand. In metalwork, I was taught on the lathe how to turn to make screw threads, and how to solder.

Father's workshop was always full of sparking plugs, carburettors and all the paraphernalia of our neighbours' mechanical problems. You can see that as I progressed through school my heart was set on producing with my hands, and that the motor vehicle fascinated me. As soon as I had finished my education at Manchester Grammar School, where I studied science as my main subject and also kept up my sports, particularly rugby and swimming, I could not wait to be apprenticed in the motor industry.

The army years brought long periods of inactivity although fortunately I managed to be associated whenever possible with vehicle spares, storekeeping, stocks and stock control. However, I had time to plan and think of my future once the war was won; and even before I left the army, thanks to a legacy left to me by a family friend in Norfolk, I was able to buy premises ready to start my chosen career and actually commenced work the day I was demobilised.

From the formation of Quinton Hazell Limited in 1946 to its takeover by Burmah Oil in 1973 I devoted my full energies to following my wartime plans. These encompassed the complete development of the motor components industry: the methods of manufacture, packaging, cataloguing and sales. In other words to make replacement components to the highest quality specification and sell at a highly competitive price. Happily, I succeeded beyond my wildest dreams. It was a bitter blow when I left the company.

I then tell of the development of a new company, the Supra Group, where once again I expanded a large motor component interest. My work throughout the years had fitted me for appointments to major public companies and bodies, where I met some wonderful people. This enabled me to discuss economics at all levels and I have tried here to outline the principles on which I have developed successful businesses and where I try to help others develop their own interests today.

My story is one of people in British industry. Throughout my life I have found a lack of understanding by governments of all parties of the vital need to develop manufacturing industry. Only when this is fully understood will Great Britain regain its place as a manufacturing nation.

CHAPTER ONE

EARLY DAYS

I was born in the Garden Village, Burnage, near Manchester, on 14 December 1920: my mother gave me the family name of Quinton – my grandmother's maiden name. My parents had settled the previous year into their first home together, on my father's return from service in the Great War of 1914–18. Home was a semi-detached house in an area just off Burnage Lane, Levenshulme, that was still almost rural. Like so many families throughout the country, my mother and father valued quiet domesticity after the years apart.

The aftermath of war remained with us. Everyone had lost brothers or friends. Many of those who returned were often seriously damaged by war: I remember one we called 'the patch man', who had lost an eye in Flanders, and used to hawk vegetables through the streets with his horse and cart. Our postman coughed and wheezed as he delivered the mail; the effects of gas never left him. My mother's sister, 'Aunt Dolly', lived with us. Like so many women in this country after 1914–18, she had been widowed during the war, and was grateful of the opportunity to share a home and help bring up her niece and nephews – perhaps spoiling them a little, in place of the children of her own that the war had denied her. Mother was a strict though fair disciplinarian, but Aunt Dolly would indulgently console me when I had been (rightly) punished, and would discreetly repair my torn shirts and trousers.

As the menfolk returned from the war, the birthrate in Burnage rose markedly. Sixty or so children were born in the village in the first years of peace. When growing up, I was never short of young friends to play with in the green fields round about. The Burnage I knew was virtually the creation of Hans Renold, the founder of Renold Chains. Swiss-born, he had come to England as a young engineer in 1873; failing to find work in London, he settled in Manchester. At first he made chains for the Lancashire textile industry, then the source of much local prosperity. With the growing popularity of the bicycle in the 1880s he developed the bush roller chain which – it is said – made the success of the bicycle possible. Renold built a new factory in central Manchester, but realising that he needed space to expand, in 1906 he bought several acres of open land at Burnage.

He was a progressive employer, and designed his single-storey factory leaving as many trees around it as possible. He also provided his workers with playing fields, and Burnage garden village was well equipped, with tennis courts, a bowling green and a village hall which I remember for the concerts and children's parties held there. The village church was St Margaret's, where I was christened and where, throughout my boyhood, my family went to services each Sunday. The housing in the village was designed to a high standard, most of the semi-detached houses in cul-de-sacs with ample gardens. Mrs Renold served on the Board of Directors. Burnage therefore offered employment and good living conditions. For local boys there was plenty of space for fun. We used to try and emulate Johnny Weismuller as Tarzan, swinging on ropes from the trees in the recreation ground. Once we built a glider, trying to fly it from the upper boughs of the biggest tree. The enterprise came to a sudden end when my friend Donald Wood broke his leg, and the grown-ups confiscated our glider.

My father, Thomas Arthur Hazell (Tom), was born in Manchester, in conditions of extreme poverty. He had educated himself out of the slums by sheer grit. He spent the Great War in India, Africa, and that part of the Middle East known then as Mesapotamia, and now Iran and Iraq. He finished his war service at Baku on the Caspian Sea, where he learnt Russian. This was of great use to him in the 1920s and 1930s when he often dealt with Russia as a timber buyer for Lloyds Sawmills of Salford, where he spent all his working life, ending as General Manager and a Director. (He used to say that he hated the Bolsheviks, but loved the Russian people.)

He met my mother, Ada Kathleen Bitton, in Manchester shortly before the war. Born in Yarmouth of solid Norfolk stock, her mother having died she had been brought up by and was living with her elder brother and his wife. Horace Bitton was then Chief Superintendent in the Manchester Post Office (it was his proud claim that the shift never finished until the last letter had been despatched).

Her father, my grandfather Ben Bitton, had a fascinating life, and as a boy I loved to listen to his stories. He started work at the age of eight, lighting fires in the boatyard to heat the water to steam the planks into shape for the making of fishing boats. Later he bought his own boat, and before the bridge over the River Yare was built, ferried passengers across from one side of Yarmouth to the other. After that he went as an apprentice baker, then bought a small baker's shop, and eventually became one of the largest master bakers in Norfolk. I believe he invented self-raising flour, and a biscuit known to this day as Norfolk Hollows. Grandfather was a truly great entrepreneur.

When I was small, we had many happy hours together. Following the death of his wife, having retired he had moved to Manchester to be close to his sons and daughters. But his yearning for the coast and the sea came through his stories, as he talked to me about Yarmouth in the 1860s when there were still old men living who had been boys on Nelson's ships at Trafalgar. Nelson's father had been Rector of Burnham Thorpe in Norfolk, and the Admiral recruited many of his crewmen in Yarmouth and the other ports of the East Coast. As a boy, I loved holidays in Yarmouth: eventually, shortly before the war, I bought a little boat and kept it there (when I went away to the war, my Uncle Fred sold it in Yarmouth, because he was sure I would be killed and never come back).

My grandfather had a great sense of history, and an even greater love of the sea. He fired me with the ambition to see the world as he had done, when he told me of travelling to America to sell his new self-raising flour: he thought New York was the most expensive city in the world, because he was charged 50 cents for a haircut.

He used to tell me about his stable of horses kept to draw the bakery delivery vans. He was justly proud that these were specially reserved for use by the local fire brigade. When a blaze occurred the firemen would go to his stable, take all the free horses, run them down to the fire station, harness them to the fire pumps, and gallop to the fire. Naturally, this took so long that nine times out of ten the building on fire had probably burnt to the ground. (It occurs to me that today, when people blame the motor vehicle for pollution, it has greatly improved the saving of life and limb in fire-fighting.)

My grandfather chose to retire at the age of 50, and although he continued to make the family's birthday, christening and wedding cakes almost until his death in 1940, he spent his last years pottering in his garden. This gave me the determination to continue working as long as I had good health.

Some of my earliest memories of my father are also concerned with horses. In his early years at the sawmills in Salford all the works deliveries were by waggons drawn by cart horses, and I well remember visiting the stables to see twenty or so magnificent dray horses. Father visited the stables every day and knew each horse by name. Their fetlocks were always combed, and hooves polished to shine as brilliantly as the harnesses; for the May Day parade, the horses themselves were brushed devotedly until they glistened. It must have been one of the saddest days of my father's life when the first motor vehicle was introduced into the works. It clearly spelt the end of the horses' usefulness, though it was to be a long time before the last horse went.

My father could get on with any animal: horses, dogs, cows (which still grazed in the fields of Burnage). I even remember him talking in a friendly way to a bull. All animals trusted him. So did people: he would help anyone. I know he had many friends, and I believe he had no enemies. I loved him dearly, and never a day goes by without my thinking of him.

He knew his job at Lloyds Sawmills from start to finish, and was very popular with his staff. His woodworking and design skills created many improvements in the joinery business. When the new Crittall metal windows became popular, my father designed wooden casements to hold them. His firm provided the window surrounds and doors for the new Manchester Corporation estates being built at Wythenshaw. At one time he had a team of men working full-time making staircases and oak panelling for boardrooms. Another speciality of the mills was the manufacture of packing cases for the export of Lancashire cotton goods. Sometimes the 'one-off' orders were very special indeed, as when packing cases were made for the despatch (by sea) of Sir Henry Segrave's racing car Golden Arrow for its successful attempt at the land speed record on Daytona Beach, Florida, in March 1929. Golden Arrow took the record with an average speed of 231.5 mph. This monster was shaped to cleave the air: it had a 1,000 horsepower aircraft engine, and huge wheels that I remember seemed to be as big as a house.

In retrospect, I am sometimes sad that my father spent so much effort and dedication in someone else's business, rather than branching out on his own. He was a superb manager. I watched him design and plan the successful future of the business of which he became a director, but always an employee and never a shareholder. Only a tiny part of his great effort ever benefited him other than at the margin. Once or twice he toyed with the idea of buying a small timber business, but with three small children (I had been joined by a sister, Dorothy, and a brother, Maurice), a house and a mortgage, I imagine that mother could not face such an uncertain future, and so he never took the decisive step.

Naturally I knew nothing of this at the time. Burnage was a wonderful place for a small boy to grow up in. When I was a small boy, milk was delivered by horse and trap, driven by the farmer's daughter Mary Norris, whose cheeks were red as ripe cherries, and who would dip pint or half-pint scoops into the shining churn, then pour the bubbling liquid into the jugs we held up to her. We spent a lot of time on the farms, where chickens walked round the farmyard pecking corn and crushed oyster shells (to ensure good eggshells). Ducks swam contentedly in the brook. Eggs were one penny each then, or a baker's dozen (13) for a shilling [5p]. They were real eggs, too, with white whites and deep amber yolks. We kept up our friendship with the farmer: when I grew older, I would gather some friends together and – long before the mechanisation of combine harvesters – we would help with the harvest, gathering the corn into sheaves and stooks, working a long day and being rewarded with a lunch of bread and cheese and a bottle of ginger beer, and sixpence at the end of the day.

In the winter, all entertainment was home-made. There were hand-wound gramophones, playing the old shellac discs with bone needles that needed sharpening and replacing, the sound emerging from large horns as on the label of 'His Master's Voice'. At the beginning of radio, we listened enthralled to crystal sets: everyone had to be quiet while we tried to tune in to listen to one of the first broadcasters from BBC Manchester, our neighbour, Mary Eastland.

At the age of five, I was sent to school. Burnage had a good elementary school run by the Manchester education authority. This was The Acacias. Miss Shepherd, my headmistress, was a strict disciplinarian (punishment was administered with a leather strap that always hung, a warning presence, on the wall behind her desk). She merely had to be in the room to ensure total attention. She was a religious zealot, but on the principle of 'a healthy mind in a healthy body' believed that scriptural knowledge should best be instilled in pupils well scrubbed with Lifebuoy soap, ensuring that all her charges were liberally cleansed with it every day. But as I recall it, she got all my class through to grammar school.

She was a fervent royalist. We said our prayers each day in front of the Union Flag. On Empire Day (24 May) our local councillor, Alderman Turnbull (who lived in Burnage Lane) visited the school to take the salute. Prayers were said for King George V and Queen Mary, for the British Empire, and paternal greetings were despatched to our cousins in Africa, Australia, Canada, Singapore, and the whole of the Empire, which we were proud to know encompassed all the many countries coloured red on the map – in those days, more than half the world. We clapped, and saluted the flag, our enthusiasm raised by the knowledge that the rest of the day would be a holiday.

We were also lucky to have Joe Coates living in the Garden Village, a fine teacher (at Alma Park Central School in Manchester) and also coach to the Manchester Boys' Football Team. He lived to better the lives of the young, on whom he had a great influence, not least in such practical ways as training in all sports. He was also a skilled masseur and thus able to ease away the pains we suffered in games of football or rugby. (In recent years it has been a pleasure to locate his son Telford Coates, now retired and living in South Australia.)

Soon I began to look forward to the annual treats of Burnage. On Guy Fawkes' Day, 5 November, there was a communal bonfire. It took two months to build, and in the lead-up weeks we boys would use the growing pile as a secret den. During the summer there were sports days on Farmer Turpin's field. There were Christmas parties in the village hall, and birthday parties too. The families of Burnage were very close, and almost every member of the community was called 'uncle' or 'auntie'.

I worked quite hard at school, and played hard, but fought for my rights. I was very strong and led fights against ruffians called the Barneys who would come over from Ladybarn and destroy our tree ropes, our bicycles and, worst of all, pillage wood from our bonfire. Sometimes my adventurousness would go too far and annoy my mother, and I would hide under a bed, from where she would flush me out with a brush and give me a no doubt deserved punishment. But she was a wonderful mother and all her children loved her.

Door-to-door deliveries to homes were still usual. Mr Jackson and his sister delivered bread. One could always hear him approaching the back door, whistling, carrying freshly baked large crusty loaves with their heavenly smell: I remember that in my early boyhood he delivered with a handcart, but his business prospered and soon he bought a motor van. The man pedalling the Walls ice-cream tricycle, blue and white and labelled 'Stop Me and Buy One', was a welcome sight in summer, and we would dash out to pay a penny for a Snofruit (a triangular block of frozen fruit juice), or (if we could afford it) twopence for a block of real creamy ice cream, which tasted better (or so my memory tells me) than anything one can buy today.

The local shops were well stocked. Our local grocers were T. Seymour Mead and John Williams & Son Limited. Their ceilings were hung with smoked back bacon and whole hams. Their counters were laden with cheeses in the round and butter cut straight from the cask, shaped into pats with wooden bats to your order. Biscuits were in large tin boxes, and were sold loose: as I fight my way into modern packaging I wonder whether the advantages of hygeine are worth the frustrations of battling with plastic.

Sometimes on Saturday morning we went to the Kingsway Cinema to see Tom Mix, Hoot Gibson or Johnny Weismuller (as Tarzan). The charge to go in was an empty earthenware marmalade jar. But many of us were keener on sports, and we would walk to Withington Baths to save money so that we could afford to pay a penny for a mug of Bovril after the swim. This, together with our summer adventures swinging like Tarzan from the trees in the recreation ground, or running, boxing or wrestling kept us boys healthily fit, even if we were often black and blue with bruises.

As I grew up, I began to understand and appreciate the remarkable and rare people who lived round us. They were a very varied group. One or two were rather eccentric, such as old Major Edleston who had fought in the Boer War in South Africa and (often) told a story of the time he was under fire when who should come up behind him but Field Marshal Lord Kitchener, who said: 'Keep your head down, Edleston, you are too valuable to get shot!' Well, perhaps.

Other neighbours were the Eastwoods, the Crowthers (Mr Crowther was a senior figure in the Co-operative Wholesale Society, that remarkable Lancashire invention), and the Wallheads. Richard Wallhead had been a Labour leader on the Manchester City Council, was Chairman of the Independent Labour Party from 1920–23, and Member of Parliament for Merthyr Tydfil 1922–32. The Lever family also lived in Burnage; one of the sons, Harold, like most bright local boys went to Manchester Grammar School, became a barrister, was MP for Manchester constituencies from 1945–79, Financial Secretary to the Treasury and (appropriately) Chancellor of the Duchy of Lancaster and (from 1979) a Life Peer as Lord Lever of Manchester.

Harold Lever became a director of the *Guardian* (in my boyhood, of course, the *Manchester Guardian*). There was another Burnage connection with that distinguished newspaper: sometimes, in Burnage Lane, we would see the impressive figure of its great editor, C.P. Scott, his noble face framed with a snow white beard, very upright, riding his Raleigh bicycle to work in Cross Street. I noticed that the chain case of his bicycle invariably gleamed with polish.

Henry Hall was to be seen in Burnage Lane walking to the stop on Kingsway to catch the tramcar to central Manchester where he was making a name with his famous orchestra: they were beginning to broadcast on the BBC from the very grand Midland Hotel.

The arts were represented in Burnage by Rendall Bond, a quiet distinguished man who was a leading sculptor, and my aunt, Alice Newland, who embroidered the most beautiful tapestries. A boyhood friend of my father's, who used to come and see us, was Harry Gilchrist – a great character, a fine singer, but best known as a successful manufacturer. He was for many years a supplier of men's braces to a promising and expanding retail company called Marks & Spencer, which was successfully opening a series of Penny Bazaars, one of them in Levenshulme. The company had moved from Leeds to Manchester in the 1890s (where the son of one of the founders, Simon Marks, attended Manchester Grammar School: later, as the distinguished head of a great firm, he was to become Lord Marks of Broughton).

Our local doctor was Dr Thompson, who had been a medical officer in the trenches of the Great War, and was devoted to the children to whom he ministered. As I remember it, all his medicines were sugared, and he insisted that the only cure for sore throats was ice cream. We were all so healthy that it was the more shocking when one lovely young girl, Joan Cotton, a good friend to many of us, went home one evening and during the night died of peritonitis; her deeply sad death, something we had not previously encountered, shocked the youngsters of Burnage who were deflated for some time afterwards.

There were other youngsters growing up in that place at that time of whom the world was later to hear much. At the Levenshulme High School for Girls was Pat Kirkwood, later to be a star in musicals on both sides of the Atlantic, and Beryl Reid (later at Withington Girls' High School), who has given audiences so much joy on the stage, radio and television.

Fun though it was to grow up in Burnage, my sights were set

wider. My father bought a car, a Swift open tourer, and on fine summer Sundays my father and mother would take us out into the Cheshire countryside. That first car, which we were thrilled to discover would do 50 miles an hour (with a good wind behind us), was an initiation into the world of the motor industry in which I was to spend my life. At the time, I recall the greatest pleasure was calling at Davenports Farm in Nether Alderley, where we would have fresh boiled eggs, thin bread and butter, home-made jam, sponge and fruit cake, all for 1s 6d [7.5p] per head.

At the age of eleven, I began to consider how I could begin in business. My home pocket money was limited – 6d a week [2.5p] from my mother and father, and a further 2d [nearly 1p] from my Aunt Dolly. After saving for six months, I bought some moulds for making lead soldiers. I 'collected' lead scrap from wherever I could find it: 'scrounged' would perhaps be a truthful word. This was then melted in a ladle over mother's gas ring and the molten metal was poured into the moulds. The result was very successful. I painted my lead soldiers, and then managed to sell them to our local toy shop, Barritts, who agreed to pay me 10d [a little less than 5p] a dozen. I then diversified into toy submarines, which (cunningly weighted) could be made to sink when placed in water, slowly rising to the surface.

I also began to buy second-hand bicycles. These normally cost me about 10s [50p] each. A quick rub-down with sandpaper, a lick of paint with a 6d tin of Woolworths lacquer, perhaps a straightening of the forks or pedals, and then I would sell them for £1 or even 25 shillings [£1.25].

My mother looked on all this with some concern. Her burning ambition was for me to receive the best schooling, to proceed to university (probably Oxford), and to obtain a secure job. In the second, I was to disappoint her.

From those years, I recall two incidents that were to have a significant impact on my future career in business. While we were not a wealthy family, like other middle-class homes between the wars we were able to afford some help in the house. My mother employed two delightful Lancashire ladies, Mrs Pollitt and Mrs Gearing, who came to our house every Friday to help with the cleaning. In the evening, when their work was done, my father would drive them home. Mrs Pollitt had a son, Harry Pollitt, who became leader of the Communist Party of Great Britain.

Young Harry and his political friends played on the understandable resentments of the workers in the depression of the Thirties. The Manchester workers were good hard-working men, but some were deluded by the Communist Party into striking for no other reason than to disrupt the country's economy. Harry Pollitt used to boast to my father that he could bring a company's workforce out on strike for no stronger reason than that there was too little sugar in the tea. This taught me always to take my employees into my confidence, setting up works committees with direct access to managing directors. In this way we stopped quarrels before they began.

The second incident in that period was at the other extreme. The British Union of Fascists, the 'Blackshirts', led by Sir Oswald Mosley, began racist attacks in Manchester, which had a large Jewish population. The Blackshirts daubed the Nazi emblem, the swastika, on the doors of Jewish businesses, broke windows and threatened thuggery in central Manchester. One day the Blackshirts organised a large rally on the road leading to London Road (now Piccadilly) station in Manchester. A mob began chanting racist slogans. Sir John Maxwell, then Chief Constable of Manchester, called in the fire brigade, coupled up the hoses, turned them on the mob and washed the ugly army down the road and under the bridge. Their bravado faded and they slunk away like drowned rats: their power in Manchester was extinguished.

These two incidents of my boyhood taught me to avoid extremes, and particularly political extremes. I remembered, too, those victims of the cruelty of the Great War, the maimed sufferers doing their brave best to earn money to keep their families: 'the patch man' who had lost his eye, the postman with his lungs damaged by gas, my Aunt Dolly who had lost her husband and her family life.

In 1931 my family moved from the garden village to the lovely country village (as it then was) of Cheadle in Cheshire. It was a pleasant place to live but then, as now, I looked back on my first eleven years as among the happiest of my life. In Burnage we had a society that was cohesive, that worked together as a team. Many of those who were boys and girls together with me in Burnage have had excellent and distinguished careers. Such was the strength of our local community and our early education at the Acacia School.

CHAPTER TWO

SCHOOLDAYS AND APPRENTICESHIP

At the age of eleven I took an entrance examination to the grammar school. Thanks to the excellent grounding from Miss Shepherd at The Acacias, and the constant encouragement of my mother and father, I was fortunate enough to be offered scholarships to Burnage High School, Chorlton Grammar School and Manchester Grammar School. Of course I elected to go to Manchester Grammar School, one of the best schools in England. The choice was made even easier since in the previous year, 1931, MGS had moved out of its old buildings in Long Millgate in the centre of Manchester. Now it occupied fine new custom-designed buildings at Rusholme in the south of the City, which meant that I was able to cycle to school from my home in Cheadle.

Though the buildings were new, they had been designed to house 950 boys: the demand for places was such that the new school opened with 1,156 pupils, and it is recorded that 'scores of applicants were turned away'. So I was well aware of my good fortune, and I look back with eternal gratitude on the education I received there. The reputation of Manchester Grammar School is such that there is no need for me to describe it at length (a recent history* relates in detail its remarkable story).

---

* *Dare to be Wise, a History of The Manchester Grammar School 1575–1990*, by Dr James Bentley: James & James, London, 1990. ISBN 0 907383 041.

The school was entirely without class. Educational excellence had no class barriers and the boy from the poorer home rubbed shoulders with those of the wealthy. We dressed alike, in grey flannels and sports jacket or blazer: school caps and ties were always worn. Common politeness was instilled into us, in simple formalities like raising one's cap to masters and elders, and giving up a seat to older people in buses and tramcars. While some boys arrived (under the eye of Jessop the porter) by bus or tram, I generally rode my bicycle to and from school in all weathers. My bicycle was a Vindec: having created a small business in repairing them, I could tell a good bike. Cycling to school meant that I could save up the daily bus fare of 9d [less than four pence] for better uses. Weather conditions were not always good. Once, in one of those thick grey fogs of winter (long before the clean air acts), when visibility was so poor that I could hardly see my bike's front wheel, I was following the tramlines and found myself inside the Fallowfield tram depot before I knew it.

One of my contemporaries, Lawrence Roy, was delivered to school daily by a chauffeured Rolls Royce (his father had built a great cinema empire). But at MGS he was treated equally with everyone else, and earned respect as a fearless goalkeeper at lacrosse: we are friends to this day.

Each morning prayers for the Gentiles were conducted in the hall by the High Master, Douglas Miller (there were 400 Jewish pupils in the school). Miller, a resplendent figure in gown and mortarboard, was perhaps less respected by many boys for his academic achievements than for the fact that he had been capped for Scotland at rugby. Another rugby international was on the staff, and very popular with the boys – Bert Toft, who had played for England, and was in charge of school rugby as well as teaching physics. Sport was an essential feature of school life: gym (in charge of Mr McCauley, who had been an Army physical training instructor), swimming, cross-country, cricket in summer, and soccer as well as rugby in winter. Swimming (coached by Mr Crawshaw) was always taken without costumes – the school was, of course, single sex – and the masters swam with the boys, who were thus encouraged to accept the naked human body as an everyday feature of life, without embarrassment.

Our masters were men of great talent who were dedicated to the boys and their education. Most teachers had several skills: Mr Radford, who taught geography, also managed the music for morning prayers. Among my teachers were Mr Twentyman for French, Ronnie Plackett for science, and Harry Lob for mathematics. Having elected to join the science stream, my subjects were English, French, mathematics, physics, chemistry, and history. All have served me well, in turn. English of course enabled me to express myself, and gave me a taste for reading that has proved a lasting pleasure. This stimulated an interest in history, particularly the development of Britain in the industrial revolution and through the nineteenth and twentieth centuries. This I continue to find fascinating. Physics and mathematics helped me throughout my business career: angles, forces and thrusts are essential knowledge in motor engineering, and a basic knowledge of maths, leading to the ability to read accounts, has proved invaluable. Fluency in French helped me greatly during the war, and for the past 30 years, with a house in France, I have been able to take a keen interest in the French people and their politics.

There was firm discipline. Lapses in work and other minor misdemeanours were punished by the staff with a firm smack on the backside with a gym shoe. But the masters were sympathetic, and accessible to our problems and difficulties, which we were encouraged to discuss until they were resolved. The good relations between masters and boys were strengthened by school camps, and 'treks' to Europe (this at a time when school visits abroad were by no means common). The admirable Harry Lob, who taught maths and was also closely involved in the organisation of school games, supervised 30 or so boys on trips to the Alps, the Mont Blanc Trek. I went in 1935: we stayed at Aix-les-Bains, and circled Mont Blanc, visiting Chamonix and camping in the gorgeous Aosta Valley, with a night staying at the University of Paris on the way back (when we managed to buy the sort of picture postcards that all schoolboys buy in Paris). As I recall it, the three-week trip cost us £15 all-in. Perhaps we did not fully appreciate at the time the dedication of teachers like Harry Lob who gave up their holidays for our education. Sadly, Lob was killed in an air-raid on Manchester.

Manchester Grammar School instilled in me the confidence to succeed. It provided me with an understanding of people in all walks of life and widely differing circumstances that has stood me in good stead throughout life. But above all, my schooldays taught me to be part of a team, educationally of a high calibre, but from wide strata of social background.

Outside school, I spent many hundreds of hours with my father in his workshop in the garden of our Cheadle home. His business was in the timber trade, but wood meant far more to him than just a living. He was a superb craftsman. In his home workshop he created fine pieces of furniture, always using English oak. He designed and made Welsh dressers, sideboards, wardrobes and chairs; all were beautiful objects to adorn the home, put together with joints so precisely and accurately formed that they scarcely needed glue when assembled. When he had finished a piece he would spend days giving it a slow french polish. I keep one of his masterpieces in my home today. He was patient, gentle and kind. He taught me some of his woodworking skills, and I still use the tools, cramps and chisels that he cherished. (He bought all his tools from John Shaw in Manchester; in his nineties, John reminisced with me about the great times he so enjoyed with my father.)

Father adapted his skills to the new world of motor vehicles. In the days when cars were a novelty, the word would go round locally: 'Ask Tom Hazell, he'll fix it'. This suited me, because my experience in repairing bicycles was developing in the direction of motor cars and their engineering. In 1936 – before I had taken my driving test, and could drive on public roads – I bought my first car. A two-seater Gordon England Sports Austin Seven, with a tapered back, it was my pride and joy. Although I had bought it from the son of my headmaster, it was not in pristine condition, and I had to change down to second gear if the wind was strong (but what more could you expect for £10?). However, after school I stripped down the engine, reground the valves, fitted new piston rings and brake shoes, put adjusters on the brake cables and finally fitted new rear springs. I then refurbished the interior and I think sold it after 18 months for £30.

My father, Thomas Arthur Hazell.
When I have to make a big decision, I sit back and think: what would father do in these circumstances? He never failed me.

Manchester Grammar School.

Elected Senior Steward of Manchester Grammar School, 1984.
Left to right: His Honour Judge Tallard, myself, and Canon Eric Saxon.

Loading export sales at the Mochdre factory, 1948.
Myself with Trevor Roberts.

Sir Gerald Nabarro and his family.

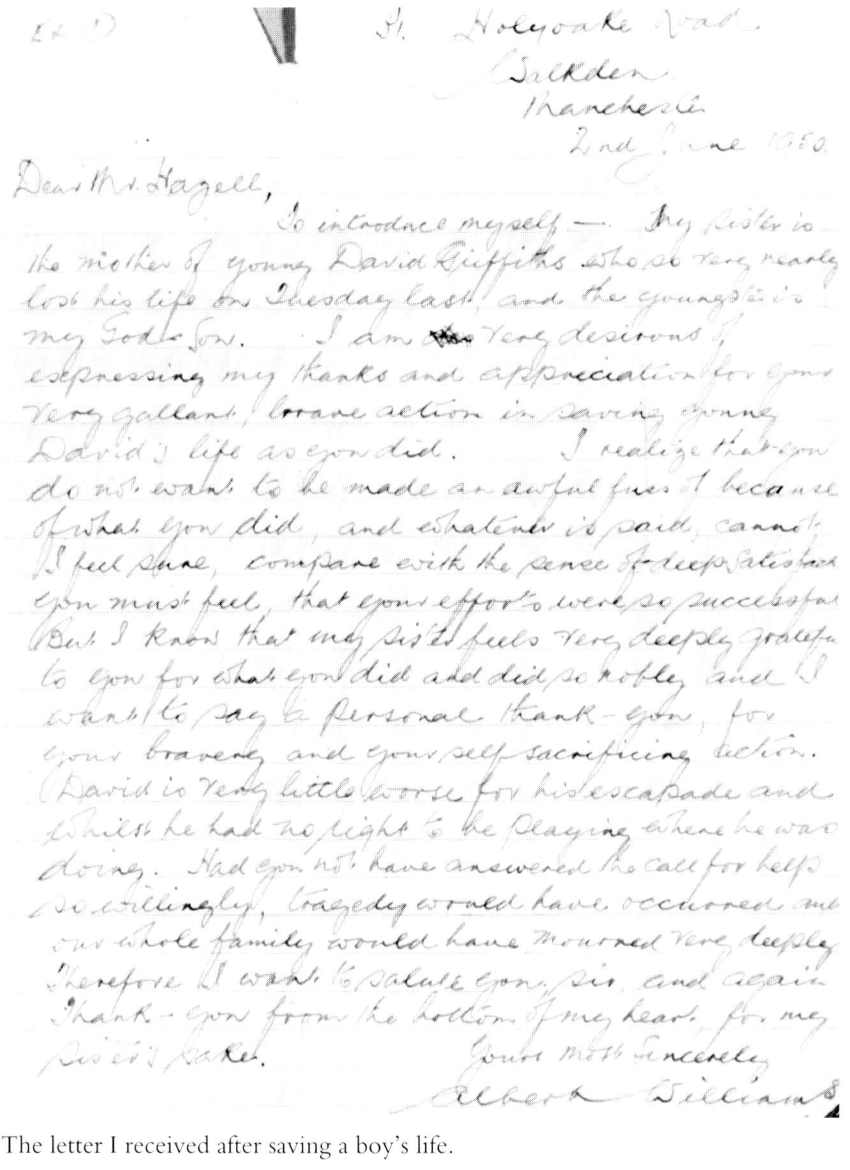

41 Holyoake Road.
Salkden
Manchester
2nd June 1950.

Dear Mr. Hagell,

To introduce myself — My sister is the mother of young David Griffiths who so very nearly lost his life on Tuesday last, and the youngster is my God-son. I am very desirous of expressing my thanks and appreciation for your very gallant, brave action in saving young David's life as you did. I realize that you do not want to be made an awful fuss of because of what you did, and whatever is said, cannot, I feel sure, compare with the sense of deep satisfaction you must feel, that your efforts were so successful. But I know that my sister feels very deeply grateful to you for what you did and did so nobly and I want to say a personal thank-you, for your bravery and your self-sacrificing action. David is very little worse for his escapade and whilst he had no right to be playing where he was doing. Had you not have answered the call for help so willingly, tragedy would have occurred and our whole family would have mourned very deeply. Therefore I want to salute you, sir, and again thank-you from the bottom of my heart, for my sister's sake.

Yours Most Sincerely
Albert Williams

The letter I received after saving a boy's life.

Mr and Mrs Tan Yew Kong, Wenna and I dining in Singapore.

Peter Dighton and I outside Quinton Hazell (Netherlands) factory, Amsterdam.

A customer's shop in Singapore.

In India—to market
Colwyn Bay products

INTENT on increasing their contribution in the drive for exports, Mr. Quinton Hazell (left), managing director of Quinton Hazell., and Mr. Geoffrey Schofield, are seen leaving the firm's Colwyn Bay factory on the first stage of their journey to India to look at the Indian market for their products and visit the new factory at Madras of Quinton Hazell (Rane) Ltd.

Flying from London Airport on Sunday, via Rome, Istanbul and Teheran, Mr. Hazell was due on Monday evening to be host at a dinner arranged in Bombay for motor traders there. For the Madras factory, which was opened last year and where large quantities of steering joints are manufactured under licence for the Indian market, the intricate machine parts and raw materials are supplied from the Mochdre factory. The remaining engineering processes, assembly and heat treatment are completed in the Indian works which are equipped with machinery entirely purpose-built in Colwyn Bay. Mr. Hazell and Mr. Schofield wanted to inspect the new assembly lines, toolroom and the production programme.

While in India they will visit customers in Calcutta as well as in Bombay and Madras, the assembly plants of British and European car and truck manufacturers, and spare-part importers to whom many thousands of Q.H.L. parts are supplied every year.

From a sales drive to be initiated for parts not manufactured by their associated company in India, the firm hope to secure a volume of business which will ensure continued employment in their factories at Colwyn Bay and Coventry.

Indian development.

Chevalier Adrien Wilputte, Managing Director of Quinton Hazell Belgium, addressing a sales conference.

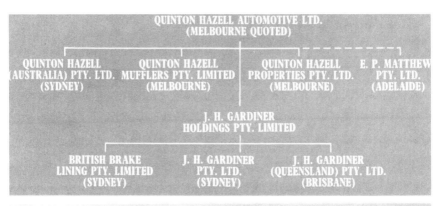

Quinton Hazell Australia Pty. The organisation chart, with a view of the silencer plant.

Stimulated by this success, I noticed an advertisement in the local paper for a 1933 model MG sports. It seemed remarkably cheap, and my first sight of it explained why. It was in a barn, and chickens had roosted in it. However, I took on the challenge. My first job was to scrub the entire car, inside and out, with soap and hot water. Once the smell had been reduced, I reconditioned the engine, had a new hood made, and fitted seals to stop oil dripping down on to the vertical dynamo. The result was satisfying, and I ran the car with great pleasure for the two years until I joined the army at the outbreak of war. No doubt it was scrapped, during the war, as valueless. Today it would be a collector's item.

My mother's ambition had been for me to stay at Manchester Grammar School until I was 18, and then go on to university. I wanted to get out into the world. A boyhood friend of my father, Robert Braid, had moved from Manchester to North Wales, where he had bought a small garage business in Abergele, on the coast between Rhyl and Colwyn Bay. That had prospered, and he had invested in a large building in Colwyn Bay that was turned into an engineering shop, in anticipation of the need to service the new motor age. The Braids offered me an apprenticeship. For me, there was no doubt that I must accept. My father saw the sense of it. My mother, as I have suggested already, was deeply upset that I should abandon what she saw as a promising academic career in favour of what she visualised as the oily setting and uncertain future of a garage. But she loved her children above everything, and only wanted them to be happy: she recognised that I was determined on this career, and so she agreed. Eventually she became very proud of the outcome, keeping a scrapbook in which she recorded the lives and successes of her three children.

So in the autumn of 1937, armed with a pair of overalls, dirty hands and an ambition to succeed, I set out on my chosen path. Correctly envisaging an enormous growth in the motor industry, I knew where I wanted to be. But at that time it was beyond my imagination that it would be my fortune, in future years, to transform the component industry.

As an apprentice to Braid Brothers in Colwyn Bay I enjoyed every hour of every day. The engineering shop had grown into a substantial business, employing about a hundred workmen. We did everything concerned with motor engineering. Because manufacturers in those days saw little need to supply spare parts, we manufactured them on demand. We stripped and rebuilt engines, gear boxes and oil pumps, and remetalled bearings. While discipline was strict and work extremely hard, the general manager, Douglas Haig, knew his job and made sure that his workmen knew theirs: I owe much to his teaching in those days. The works foreman, Vic Williams – seldom seen without his bowler hat – made certain that we were taught every aspect of engineering.

From time to time I was asked to help out at the Braid Brothers Garage in Deganwy, four miles to the west of Colwyn and overlooking Conway Bay, and across to Anglesey. The Deganwy garage was managed by Norman Braid. At the age of 18 I was made Assistant Manager at Deganwy, which had a staff of ten. So while still an apprentice and learning engineering skills from excellent workmen, I was given responsibility for costing, repairs, stock control in the small stores, and the accounts. I knew I was making progress and thrived on hard work and responsibility.

There were two reasons in particular why I was glad to be working in Deganwy. I was lodging in that little town in a boarding house run by Mr and Mrs Owen and their family (and paying 25 shillings [£1.25p] per week, including laundry, breakfast and evening meal). Secondly, while I was in the garage one day, an extremely pretty girl brought her car in for servicing. I discovered that she was Morwenna Parry-Jones, daughter of Morris Parry-Jones, an eminent sheep judge, a farmer and butcher with shops in Deganwy and Conway. On that first occasion I merely registered that she was obviously a charming girl, and well educated (at Howell's School, Denbigh, that most distinguished of girls' schools in the area). I have been told that I was a well set-up young man; still a keen rugby-player, I kept myself fit. On one of Miss Parry-Jones's later visits to the garage, we got into conversation. Soon we were going out together, and Wenna (as everyone called her) became an essential part of my life. (My fellow-lodger at Deganwy was Peter Finch, who was to marry Wenna's great friend Edith Harnden; he was a fine man and died too young.)

Other activities claimed my time. In 1938, with other friends of my age who could see that a war to stop Hitler and his Nazi ambitions was soon to become inevitable, I joined the Territorial Army, becoming a member of the 61st Medium Regiment, Royal Artillery, the Denbighshire Yeomanry. Its headquarters were in Colwyn Bay, and the regiment was equipped as a 6-inch Howitzer unit.

Another incident from that period taught me a healthy disrespect for 'the authorities'. In 1938 the Royal Navy submarine *Thetis* was accidentally sunk in Liverpool Bay, off Point Lynas, Anglesey, with considerable loss of life. Like many people in the area, Wenna and I went to the top of the Great Orme in Llandudno from which it was possible to see the prow of the tragic vessel sticking clear of the water. With everyone else, we felt the frustration of not being able to help.

In the garage at Deganwy, one of the mechanics, Jack Davies, and I were shocked that life could be lost so easily. We thought about the problem from an engineering perspective, and designed a crude escape apparatus with an air inlet and exhaust pipe to the surface, worked by a compressor. We submitted plans to the Admiralty. We were told that the whole scheme was ridiculous and not worth considering. (During the war, we were not pleased to discover that the Schnorkel, a breathing-tube installed by the Germans in their submarines, was a refined development of the concept that Jack Davies and I had submitted to the Admiralty in 1938.)

On 29 August 1939, not yet 19, as a Territorial soldier I was called to the colours, a few days before war was declared on 3 September. I began what was to prove to be six years service in the army. Soon afterwards, I found some irony in the fact that the Braid Brothers engineering works in Colwyn Bay was turned over to making aircraft parts for the duration, and its workmen were thereafter in a 'reserved occupation', which meant that they were not liable to call-up for active service. Had I not volunteered for the territorials I would no doubt have spent the war in Colwyn Bay.

CHAPTER THREE

THE WAR

On 3 September, the Sunday morning when Britain declared war on Germany, I was in the Quarter Master's Stores of our Territorial headquarters in Colwyn Bay, sorting out uniforms, breeches, boots, and flat peaked hats. Most of our equipment was 25 years old, and dated from the 1914–18 War. Our guns were of that age: 6-inch Howitzers (the name comes from the German for sling or catapult), which fired 100 lb shells on a high trajectory. They were mounted on frames with big wheels bound with metal. Originally they had been horse-drawn, but in 1939 we were issued with huge Scammel tractors which did a marvellous job.

The common belief was that we must prepare for an imminent German attack (there was an air raid warning over London shortly after the declaration of war, though it turned out to be a false alarm). But for the first few days, there was a feeling of urgency, and a willingness to put up with discomfort in the cause of the war. Within a few days of mobilisation we were ordered to Denbigh, and taking over all the empty premises in the town we bedded down on palliasses filled with straw, and tolerated the terrible food produced by the Territorial cooks, whose experience of cooking before call-up was evidently limited to perhaps occasionally boiling an egg. From Denbigh we moved to Chippenham where the whole population welcomed us with open arms. But soon we were practising on the firing ranges of Larkhill Camp on Salisbury Plain, and then sailing from Southampton to Cherbourg as part of the British

Expeditionary Force (BEF) to France. Then we made our way down the Cherbourg peninsula to Le Mans and thence north to Arras, in the Pas de Calais.

There was no fighting: Hitler had made a pact with the Soviets, who were consolidating their military occupation of the Baltic states. We found ourselves in what soon became known as the 'phoney war', seeing no military action. But the winter of 1939–40 was bitterly cold. On our way across France we were billeted in open barns, pigstys and other farm buildings, all without sanitation or running water. Everything froze; Tommy Waterworth put on his woollen balaclava helmet at new year and it had to be virtually cut off for Easter. Life was hard: and living among the cemeteries of the 1914–18 war was not too encouraging.

Nevertheless our Regiment of 800 men was first class. Despite starting off with very little training, there was great enthusiasm, and the presence of Regular Army officers and non-commissioned officers soon brought us up to pitch. Lieutenant Mantle looked after our lines near Douai, where we lived in a large sugar warehouse shared with about 1,000 rats. Mantle prepared shooting parties, but we never really overcame the problem. The sugar factory maintained a fleet of American-built trucks, veterans from the 1914–18 war, to carry the sugar beet from the fields. Naturally, no spare parts could be obtained, and every component had to be made in the factory's very efficient workshop. I was in my element.

Our main gun positions were at Champsfleur on the Belgian border. We spent many months of the 'phoney war' digging gun emplacements and service trenches for ammunition dumps. This was in line with the conventional military strategy of the allies, British and French, most of whose generals were still influenced by the static trench warfare of the first world war. This was particularly true of the French, who believed themselves to be secure behind the Maginot Line, a system of forts linked by underground passages, running the length of the German border north to south.

During those early months of 1940 life in France for the British soldier was boring and routine. But on Friday nights those not on guard or special duties were allowed a visit into the nearest town in the army's 'passion wagons'. We went to Le Mans, Arras, Douai and

Lille. There were visits to rather interesting bars and cabarets. Famous variety stars and singers, among them Vera Lynn and Gracie Fields, came out to give much appreciated army concerts. A four-course dinner and a nice bottle of wine could be enjoyed in a good hotel for 4s 6d [22.5p] English money – then about 36 French Francs. Once a week we organised soccer and rugby matches. Our Lieutenant Quarter Master was Frank Hislop, a regular officer of great courage and sincerity. Other companions from those days remain friends: I think of Major Vaughan Richards, Lieutenant-Colonel Tom Leathes and Captain Sid Cutler MC, among many others who join us at reunions and with whom we remember the good experiences. The mists of time dull the losses and fear.

Then in May 1940 the 'phoney war' ended. Hitler's troops began to sweep westwards. On 13 May, Winston Churchill became Prime Minister, and announced to the House of Commons that he had 'nothing to offer but blood, toil, tears and sweat'. In the days that followed, we were to see plenty.

A few days earlier we had been ordered north into Belgium to oppose the German advance. Unfortunately, we had dug our guns into semi-permanent emplacements. Now we had to extract them and become mobile again. At the same time, the French high command was discovering the uselessness of the much-vaunted Maginot line, as the Germans, using air power with devastating efficiency, simply flew their airborne forces into north-west Europe. The order came to retreat to the coast. The village streets were packed with bombed vehicles and dead and dying horses making the roads impassable. Abandoning our vehicles we began the 40-mile walk to the coast at Dunkirk. It was on that march, laden with tin hat, gas mask and rifle, that I first damaged my instep; it seemed to recover, but problems with it were to manifest themselves four years later.

When about half-way to Dunkirk, I was crossing a field when I was taught an unforgettable lesson. A shell came over and hit an Army post office. Thousands of Francs flew into the air and rained down upon us. As I was about to run forward and pick up the booty, the soldier in front of me was shot, and fell dead. In an instant, money became unimportant. Since then I have never forgotten that life is the most important possession. Not everyone was so sensitive: five miles further on I came across a gunner carrying, with some difficulty, a very large marble-cased clock.

When we arrived on the sea-front at Dunkirk, the town was ablaze. Oil storage tanks belched huge plumes of black smoke and the flames made night into day. I tried to walk out into the sea to one of the boats offshore, but the water was covered with a thick layer of diesel oil which covered the bottom of my battledress trousers and burnt my legs. Back on shore, I was amazed to see one of our subalterns, Lieutenant Charles McLaren (later Lord Aberconway), complete with Howitzer and tractor. How he got them there I will never know, but he did, and I was very proud of my regiment.

The discipline of the troops was magnificent, although no one knew what was happening, or whether we would be taken off. There were ships offshore, but no way of reaching them, and no air cover at that stage: in any case, we could see many of them ablaze and sinking. Yet as the battle raged around us, we were confident that the Navy would get us off – and they did. Meanwhile we were marched backwards and forwards from Dunkirk to Bray-Dunes and De Panne each day, with no food other than a tin of condensed milk. There was even some humour: one night we were sheltering in a bomb crater on the beach when one of the men lit a cigarette. A subaltern ordered him to douse it, giving him a lecture to the effect that the night sights on German aircraft were so good that they could pick out the rank of senior officers, and bomb them. In chorus, the men shouted: 'Just the buggers they want to bomb!'

For two or three days I shared a shell-hole with a very amiable solicitor (in civilian life) who was in charge of headquarters records. He was sure that he was going to be killed. He insisted that I learnt his army number, to report to his relatives when I got back to England, and he repeated it over and over again: Sergeant Hough A.G. 924483. (How he expected me to remain alive, when we were together in the shell hole, I never understood.)

Gradually the Royal Navy, assisted by a flotilla of small boats crossing and re-crossing the Channel from England, took the men off. Our group was assembled on the beach and marched the full length of the mole until we could jump down on to the deck of the destroyer HMS *Malcolm*. I was directed down a series of ladders and found myself in the ammunition hold. Having watched destroyers and warships being blown up in the previous days, I forced my way back up the ladders and eventually finished the trip on the fly bridge. We had a few stray machine gun bullets through the canvas, but no casualties. As we crossed the Channel the sea was dotted with the masts of ships sunk during the operation. Occasionally the funnel of a larger vessel bobbed disconsolately in the calm water. 'Operation Dynamo', the evacuation from Dunkirk, began on 27 May, and the last men were brought off on 3 June: 860 ships took part, and well over 300,000 men were brought back to England.

On arrival at Dover, we were put on to a train for Dorchester. Of that journey, I remember only two details: as I got into the carriage, there was Sergeant Hough A.G. 924483 (alive) – and the gunner with the marble clock. Once at Dorchester Barracks, I believe I slept for 48 hours, only waking at mealtimes. New battledress, socks and shirts were issued, and we were then allowed into the town. My first thought was to send a telegram to my girlfriend Wenna, and to my mother, telling them that I was safe and well and in England. Then I went to a barber, and asked for a haircut and shampoo. He took one look at the dirt, sand and diesel in my hair and refused to touch me. Rather forcefully, I explained the reason I was in that condition, whereupon his attitude changed spectacularly: afterwards he refused to accept payment.

Most of the British Expeditionary Force had, amazingly, returned unharmed. But of course most heavy equipment, and for us that meant our heavy guns, had been left behind. Meanwhile the German armies were poised on the coast of mainland Europe preparing, as most people believed, for the invasion of the British Isles. There was no time for relaxation. Our regiment was re-formed and stationed in the East Riding of Yorkshire at Fridaythorpe, half way between York and the coast. Because of my experience in handling stores, I was promoted in one day from Bombardier to Battery Quarter Master Sergeant – at the age of 19, the youngest in the British Army. My military stores was in build-ings belonging to a farming family, the Coopers: they were generous and kind to all of us. It was a particular joy when Wenna came over from Wales to visit us.

While we waited for the replacement of our heavy guns, which had been left behind in France (despite the efforts of young Lieutenant McLaren), we were expected to destroy the invading hordes with five rounds of .303 ammunition per man, and Molotov cocktails (beer bottles filled with petrol and tar) which we were instructed to ignite with a match and then hurl at German tanks as they came up the road. Charabancs (buses) had been requisitioned to give our troops mobility, and to carry us to the expected German landing zones.

One night there was an alert. My staff and I issued five rounds to every man and in pitch darkness, sitting in the charabancs, we listened for the noise of aeroplane engines and waited for the order to move against the enemy. Suddenly there was the crack of a rifle. It was generally believed that parachutists must be landing on top of us. But no movement orders were given. Nothing more happened. As daylight broke, we could see a hole in the bus roof – made by a bullet fired from inside. Nobody volunteered as having fired the shot. Every man handed back five bullets into the store. On one occasion we witnessed a daylight raid by German bombers on Driffield aerodrome. Our defence battery at Bridlington disabled one of the raiders and the plane crashed on the beach.

It was many months before new guns arrived. The interval was not unpleasant for me: I was playing rugby both for my Regiment and for the Army Division. Those who were chosen for the Army were granted an additional 48 hours leave, and so there was real competition to be selected for the team. My time in Yorkshire, despite the war, was very happy. In 1941 we were in Ripon, a beautiful town where, despite the blackouts and wartime restrictions, historic tradition was maintained. At 9 o'clock each night the Town Crier would come into the town square and call, once in each of four directions, 'Nine o'clock and all's well'. It struck me as typical of the indomitable British spirit.

After being stationed in Hunmanby, near Filey, and Tickhill, near Doncaster we had a long stint in Ackworth Moor Top, which introduced me to the warmth of the Yorkshire mining community. My billet was a semi-detached cottage, and my landlords were Mr and Mrs Dyson, with their son Frank (then about eleven) and their daughter Linda. Edith Dyson could make marvellous meals out of virtually nothing, and lunch would start with the traditional huge Yorkshire pudding soaked with rich gravy.

The Beverley Arms at Ackworth Moor Top, with Madge and Molly as joint licensees, became in effect our Regimental Mess, offering kindness and hospitality as fast as the beer was drawn. In that community, everyone helped everyone else. I learnt about the lives of the miners we met in the Beverley Arms. The miners were poor people, receiving very little money for their dangerous life. But as they depended on each other for their safety down the pit, so their families depended on each other on the surface, and lived in complete harmony. Every month the free ton of coal was delivered: that was part of their reward. Tired men home from the pit, together with their wives, shovelled most of the coal into the coalhouse, but some would be shared with neighbours who, in turn, performed acts of kindness – haircutting, baking loaves, collecting children from school, looking after the retired and the sick. I have never seen so many kindnesses shown in a small community. Each night the fire would be banked up with coal so that there was always hot water for the ritual wash taken in a tin bath before the fire in the living room.

The life was a hard one. The miner would be up early (usually before it was light, in the winter). Then there would be a long cold trip by bicycle and after the descent a walk of a mile to the pit face. The coal was hacked out by pick and shovel: there was little mechanisation in those days. Once I did a trip down to the pit face to witness the difficulties. I would never have wished to work in a mine, but after half a shift I was absolutely sure that I would never go down a mine again.

The miners drank heavily; but in the course of a shift down the pit, a miner would lose up to three-quarters of a stone in weight. I have always felt that the miner's pints replaced this lost fluid: six pints of beer a night was the norm for many men, and almost a necessity. They were allocated special rations during the war, but their wages were too low to buy enough of the good food that was available.

I am still in touch with the Dyson family, my hosts in Ackworth Moor Top. Linda lives there to this day. Frank found work in the railway wagon works at Doncaster as a joiner. Later he took an external degree at Leeds University. In his early days he borrowed a small amount of money from me to buy a field and rear chickens. Showing courage and foresight, he soon found that his skills with timber enabled him to build houses. His entrepreneurial approach quickly secured him customers, and he was away. Today, as a member of Lloyds, he runs a successful insurance and investment business in Wakefield.

Throughout my war service Morwenna Parry-Jones and I had kept in touch. Sadly, her father had died in May 1940 when I was in France, but her mother kindly encouraged our friendship. She was a wonderful lady who, born in Lancashire at Oldham, had completely assimilated to the Welsh way of life and preferred the Welsh language to her native English. So we always called her 'Nain' (Welsh for 'grandmother'). She backed me to the hilt in my great plans for life with Wenna once the war was over.

In 1942 the main action of the war was on the Russian front, and in North Africa (where preparations were then being made for what became a great British victory at Alamein). Those of us remaining in Britain were kept busy training for the forthcoming invasion of Europe; but it was possible to take leave from time to time. So on 26 September 1942, Wenna and I were married at the Parish Church in Deganwy, North Wales. Wenna found the clothing coupons for a very smart going-way outfit, and I wore a new battledress with my Battery Quarter Master Sergeant's insignia. My best man was Bernard Gilchrist, my friend from boyhood in the Garden Village of Burnage, and at Manchester Grammar School. My brother-in-law John Holt representing the family, gave Wenna away. He wore the battledress of a Company Sergeant Major (after the war he was to become a senior manager with the Phoenix Assurance Company). It was a tremendous display of supportive family unity.

After the ceremony, Wenna and I were driven in an open landau to a reception at the Castle Hotel, Conway. It was a glorious day, with the first snow glistening on Snowdon, and the sun shimmering on Conway river (where soon afterwards the floating 'Mulberry harbours' were assembled, to be towed to the French coast for D-day). After the wedding breakfast and the speeches, and Wenna's mother had stuffed some new crisp £5 notes into my pocket, we were driven to the station and locked in an old-fashioned railway carriage for the journey to Chester where we were to spend our first night.

We had cleared away the confetti by the time the train arrived at Chester, and when we went in to dinner were convinced that we looked exactly like any other young married couple taking a rare weekend's leave. But then, during dinner, a page came into the dining room and loudly requested 'the newly-married couple' to take a telephone call. We walked out to the applause of the rest of the diners, to find that the caller was my brother-in-law, John, playing a prank on us. On the next day we went down to Oxford, staying at the Mitre Hotel and spending several days in leisurely walks round the colleges and gardens. I could not help wondering where my life would have led if I had pursued a university career as my mother had wished. Finally, we went on to a couple of nights in London before I returned to my regiment. Half a century later, I can only be grateful that Wenna has backed every move in my career, and that we still plan new challenges and test new ideas.

Back to the war. After a long trek to the north of Scotland, we were based in the tiny fishing village of Avoch on the Cromarty Firth. Here again, as in Yorkshire, the people were so kind. We were there for Christmas and Hogmanay and every door was open as we 'first-footed' after midnight at New Year: there was a dance with fiddles and bagpipes in the village hall.

Then we moved south-east to Huntly in Aberdeenshire. After many months of uncertainty, as the fighting took place in North Africa and the prospect of an invasion of Britain receded, a purpose was added to our training. We were being trained as mountain troops to develop a 'second front', an invasion of Europe through Norway. We spent every day in the mountains, practising landings on the cliffs in all weathers. Exercises were regularly carried out climbing the cliffs under fire from live ammunition, making sure you kept your bottom into the cliff, and not sticking out. At first we believed that the live rounds were probably about a yard behind us, until one of us – Johnny Sutherland – took a shot right through his waterbottle. From then on, we all froze to every boulder and stayed squashed against the rocks, which was better for one's health but poor for one's love-life. We learnt to construct igloos from the ice, to cut away under the base of a pine-tree and build a snow wall inside which we could be warm and comfortable. We were trained by Norwegian instructors, experts in mountain skills and also ski-ing; they were fantastic.

In whatever spare time we had, we made private expeditions into the magnificent Scottish countryside and, using camouflage nets, secured some fine salmon and trout. These provided a rare treat after the emergency rations of corned beef and pemmican, the latter a confection made of dried meat pounded with fat and flavoured with currants: it kept for years, was said to be very nutritious, and tasted utterly foul. Off duty, there seemed to be no rationing in that part of Scotland and we were offered so much meat, eggs and chocolate that we thought we were in heaven. The Church Elders were even persuaded to allow films to be shown to the troops on Sundays, an unprecedented happening in Scotland at that time. But the training was hard, and this slight relaxation of moral discipline on a Sunday kept the boys' spirits up.

After all this, the decision was taken not to mount a 'second front' through Norway. That was fortunate for us. The cost in lives would have been horrific. With replacement guns we therefore began a series of exercises that tested our spirits to the limit. Firing camps were held at Otterburn in Northumberland where the new streamlined shells gave us an extra 1500 yards range. Fitness for the whole Regiment, involving a four-mile run each morning, coupled with complete gunnery efficiency was the order of the day. Finally we were issued with the new 5.5 guns ready for the D-day invasion. The invasion was to be in Northern France, and so my regiment moved to Aldershot to make preparations. Throughout the war years in England and Scotland I had played a great deal of rugby football and represented the Army Division in many matches. At this point, ironically for one who had always prided himself on fitness, my foot (which had been injured on the way to Dunkirk) deteriorated to the point where, in spite of wearing an arch support, I was declared unfit and graded B7 – Home Service only.

So, after five years with all my friends in the Denbighshire Yeomanry, I was posted as Battery Quarter Master Sergeant (BQMS) in 4th Field Training Regiment, Royal Artillery, at Larkhill Camp, Salisbury Plain. I was appointed Mess Treasurer. My Commanding Officer, Peter Walton (who had been a master at Norwich School) asked me to sort out the muddle in the Quarter Master's Stores. The records were months out of date. There was a shortage of blankets, towels, shirts and so on – their value was, of course, as good as coinage in those days. But worst of all the ammunition count was inaccurate, and the logbooks on the tanks showed a deficit of 25,000 gallons of petrol.

As a recall it, a general inspection was due in about six weeks; and by then everything had to be in apple-pie order. We worked day and night using every trick in the book known to old soldiers. The audit was subsequently completed satisfactorily. The Company Commander was duly grateful and provided me with ample leave. I was therefore able to return home to North Wales at weekends to keep an eye on my late father-in-law's business. I did these trips on a Triumph Tiger motorcycle and in winter very often arrived in Deganwy frozen stiff.

Some odd things happened at Larkhill. The place seemed immune to the laws of chance. The 4th Field Training Regiment provided special gunnery practice for all ranks on a six week cycle, in preparation for posting overseas. Each new intake was offered, by the permanent staff of gunners, a prize of a brand new bicycle. Such a bicycle was shown to each intake, and raffle tickets were duly sold. It is very strange, but in my 18 months at Larkhill, the same bicycle was won every time by the permanent staff, and turned up again ready for the next intake.

Following the launching of the invasion of Europe on D-day, 6 June 1944, Salisbury Plain became a hive of military activity in all directions. Many paratroop regiments, and also the glider brigade that carried some of them, were stationed there. On some days the skies would be full of Dakota aircraft as the paratroops left to make landings in Europe. Often when they returned a few days later, they would be carrying all sorts of trophies. These included goods from collapsible bicycles to gold watches, a grand piano from a German officers' mess, and even a beautiful open Mercedes staff car. Most were 'lost' in clouds of secrecy.

More very strange things happened. There was a Czechoslovakian in our unit, who had anglicised his name to 'Bert Light'. I could never fathom what he was supposed to be doing. However, one day he told me in strict secrecy that Hermann Goering's stamp collection would be arriving at Amesbury that evening, and that he had orders to take charge of it. This was not as improbable as it might seem, since throughout the war there was an underground trade in stamps: our agents throughout Europe would bring back the latest issues, which were prized. At this stage of the war, I could scarcely credit the story of Goering's stamp collection. But when we reached the airport, the collection had apparently been picked up by someone else. We spent the next seven hours chasing every lead, but eventually concluded that the collection had changed hands several times before the end of the day.

The war in Europe officially ended on 8 May 1945. I was in Larkhill. The realisation of the coming of peace, after six years of loss of life and the imposition of so many restrictions, led to an explosion of relief and joy. As Quarter Master I could only watch as my careful accounting was torn to shreds and blackout screens and spare beds were thrown on to a huge bonfire. Cordite bags were broken open and the sticks of cordite thrown on to the flames. Every available Very-light cartridge was fired. The Mess was drunk dry. My one worry was how to account for all this. I need not have worried: the Army, for once considerate of our jubilation, turned a blind eye to the whole episode. For a few months more we devoted our attention to training for the war with Japan that continued in the Far East. That ended with the dropping of atom bombs on Hiroshima and Nagasaki, and the subsequent surrender of Japanese forces on 2 September.

For those of us awaiting demobilisation, there were several months in which we had hours to think and plan our future. I used this time to refine the plans that had been in my head since those early days in the Braids engineering shop at Colwyn Bay.

When, in spring 1946, I was demobilised in Oldham – not too far from Manchester, where I had been born 25 years before – I started work the same afternoon.

CHAPTER FOUR

STARTING A BUSINESS

In my last year as Battery Quarter Master at Larkhill I had close contact with the American forces, and particularly with the Quarter masters of their Motor Transport Department. I was able to compare the practices of the two systems (while at the same time greatly improving my personal comfort by adding American Army shirts to my wardrobe). When we ordered components for British Army vehicles, the individual parts for an assembly would consist of up to 20 different part numbers; the components would arrive wrapped in black grease and paper from the suppliers, and very seldom were all necessary components provided in the same delivery. This led to delays and disruption. In contrast, the American Army either provided the complete assembly ready-made, or at least boxed all necessary components together. For example, headlamps were supplied as a complete integral unit, including the bulb: fitting could be done by inexperienced personnel in a matter of minutes. Similarly, there were exchange gearboxes, back axles, steering assemblies, dynamos, starters, and ready-lined brake shoes, provided complete and only requiring to be fitted.

I saw that this principle could be equally successful in civilian life. I determined that after demobilisation I would manufacture, pack and market motor components in complete sets, clean and well labelled. The prospect was so exciting that I wanted to start straight away; and indeed during 1945 while waiting to be demobilised (the war in Europe ended on 8 May), on my leaves from Larkhill at

Deganwy I planned the new business. Towards the end of 1945, with excellent advice from my father and my brother-in-law John Holt, and with great encouragement from my mother-in-law and Wenna, I purchased a property in Mochdre, to the west of Colwyn Bay, towards Llandudno Junction. This was Mochdre Garage, a substantial garage with a large hall above, which was to be our first workshop.

Once I was demobilised, starting a business from a very small capital base (£5,000, with the garage premises as collateral for a limited overdraft) was probably the most exacting experience of my working education. I had a fine grounding in engineering before the war, thanks to the sound teaching of the Braid brothers: during the war I continued to refurbish components and motor cycles whenever there was spare time during my army service. By chance I had also served as Mess Treasurer, which had given me a basic insight into the principles of accounting: fortunately, however, Wenna as Company Secretary from the first day saw to the general running of our business accounts. She also controlled the debtors' ledger with a rod of iron, for which I shall always be grateful.

When you start a new business it is no use saying 'I am going to sell . . .' or 'I am going to manufacture . . .' without detailed consideration. It is essential to understand your outlay and liabilities, within a planned budget. From the start, costs have to be known and recorded. Cash flow is absolutely vital and it is essential that payment terms are strictly enforced. Many companies will try to extend the payment of monthly accounts to new enterprises, but you must start the way you intend to go on. My basic rules of business have never changed: despite a fluctuating bank interest rate, the relationship of sales and gross profit must be kept in line.

The first challenge was to find things to make: the second was to sell them. In 1946 the popular universal joints were almost impossible to buy. I found that several of these were to be found in each British aircraft: such aeroplanes were at that time being scrapped at airfields all over the country, and working parts, including items such as the universal joint, were being thrown away. I concluded a deal to buy every such joint throughout the United Kingdom. On one purchasing trip to Northern Ireland I watched brand new aeroplanes being pushed out of the manufacturer's hangar, take off and fly one circuit of the airfield, come down to earth and taxi to one side ready to be scrapped. So the components were virtually new.

We devised a machine for stripping these out of the housing, repacked them and began selling them. At the same time, we devised a machine for taking individual cells out of batteries, and John and Orlando Oldham of Oldham Batteries, together with the proprietors of Tungsten Batteries, let me have some new plates and separators so that, having extracted the dud cells, we could rebuild the batteries. Although the batteries we sold then were not new, they put back on the road many pre-war cars that had been propped up on bricks in garages for the duration of hostilities. The goods we sold were in short supply, and soon led to a very good business, earning Quinton Hazell Limited a reputation as a quality supplier. Yet despite the acute shortage of such components in the trade, sales to established wholesalers were very difficult.

In 1946 pricing, purchasing and sales policy in the motor industry was totally governed by a limited number of component suppliers, working in tandem with the motor manufacturers. Wholesalers, behind their drab green windows, were tied hand and foot. Discounts were minimal, so as not to conflict with the main motor agents and distributors. To become a wholesaler, and eligible to be supplied by the component manufacturers, you had to apply for membership of the Society of Motor Manufacturers and Traders (SMM&T). You had to have a turnover (I believe it was £20,000 a year then, probably equivalent to £200,000 today) which may seem very small in today's terms: but an aspiring applicant, as a Factor, was excluded because none of the specialist manufacturers would supply him, and therefore even £20,000 turnover was unattainable. So, in theory, no one could join the club. I had observed this closed shop in action while an apprentice before the war; I knew how it worked. I now decided that the way to break the stranglehold was to manufacture products where demand was greatest and supply most limited: in other words, to challenge the companies with the softest underbelly.

There was another problem. To manufacture, of course we needed steel. In those years of shortage after the war, there was no allocation of steel for new enterprises: established companies had first priority, and no supplies were left for those trying to start up manufacturing businesses. I wrote many letters to those responsible for allocating steel supplies: all returned a blank refusal. Finally, I received a letter from the Ministry of Supply in London, saying that there was no way a returned soldier could qualify for a steel licence. In other words, those who had produced during the war were allowed to maintain the status quo, while those who had been away from home on other business were not to be rewarded.

With the letter in my pocket, I went to London. Entering the office of the lady Controller of Steel Allocation at the Supply Ministry in Shell Mex House, I explained that my call was simply out of politeness, as I was in fact on my way to the *Daily Express* down the road in Fleet Street to expose this scandalous treatment of an ex-serviceman. Having risked life and limb as a mere soldier throughout the war, I was now being told that this debarred me from a steel allocation because I had not contributed to wartime manufacture. (At that time, the *Daily Express* was featuring stories of unfair treatment of returned veterans, particularly those with the 1939–45 Star.) I was promptly given coffee and biscuits, and asked to return immediately to North Wales where my steel licence would be with me the next morning. True to the lady Controller's word, the steel licence arrived by the first post, and in a short time our planned programme of serious manufacturing began.

We had by this time produced, if in rather simple form, a catalogue showing the various items we could offer. They included a range of road springs, particularly (I remember) for the Morris 8 Series E, and the Y Model Ford (a transverse spring providing an early version of independent suspension): these were rebuilt by the local blacksmith in Mochdre. We also listed parts for most of the range of pre-war and immediate post-war cars, including the Standard 8, 10 and 12, the Morris 10 and 12 and the Vauxhall. All the cars we serviced were British (apart from the occasional American Chrysler or Buick, there were hardly any imported foreign vehicles in those days). The commercial vehicles on the road were Austin, Leyland, Morris, Ford and Bedford.

Geoff Gostage ran Mochdre Garage on his own account as

distributor for Singer Cars: he also enthusiastically repaired and put back on the road many vehicles that had been laid up throughout the war. Meanwhile I developed the hall above the garage as an engineering shop, racked out with stocks of essential motor components. We had one or two centre lathes, a milling machine, drills, and lots of enthusiasm. Everything had to be carried up 25 steps – machinery, steel and all other requirements. One morning I carried a hundredweight in each hand up the steps to prove to my staff how easy it was: example is the best incentive. During those early years I had to lead from the front. I suppose I never changed. Be it working a machine, packing, selling, or collecting an account, I was prepared to do everything even down to cleaning a blocked drain or carrying steel bar or forgings.

With our limited steel allocation we manufactured a range of king pins and bushes to cover a similar range of vehicles. We thwarted the vehicle manufacturers by making complete sets – two king pins, four bushes, thrust washers or races, cotter pins and nuts, neatly wrapped and packaged in an attractive Quinton Hazell bag with the Welsh Dragon emblem. (We registered that design, which was to prove particularly useful in the Far East at a later stage.) Finally, the pack was put into a cardboard box which also bore the Dragon insignia, and was clearly labelled on the box end. At this time the vehicle manufacturers were still packing each item separately in sticky greasy paper, and very often could not supply the complete set of parts needed for a full assembly.

We continued to re-assemble and package our universal joints and manufactured axle shafts. We also set up a department where we rebuilt dynamos and starters, and were one of the first companies to offer an exchange system on these items, buying in stocks from wherever we could find them. We bought armatures from Woods of Huddersfield, and bearings and bushes from Remax of London (a company we subsequently purchased). After refurbishing, the completed unit was then exchanged in an over-the-counter swap. Such ingenuity was necessary in those early days.

Money was desperately short, and financial control was essential. Wenna looked after that rigorously. At the beginning we worked out a minimum daily turnover at a fixed gross profit of $33^{1}/_{3}\%$; after expenses we were left with a net profit of about 8%. Overdrafts were at the sensible price of 6% in those days, but making sure that the daily turnover figure was achieved was vital, and the collection of monthly accounts was pursued with vigour. If we fell short of our target one day, it was carried forward to the next, striking a weekly and a monthly balance. This was sound basic common sense; but it was essential, then as now, in order to keep a company afloat.

In that first year we were diverted briefly from all this when, on 31 October 1946, our son Morris was born. He was the greatest delight, but in his first months suffered from a stomach problem so that he could only digest goats' milk. So in the terrible winter of 1946–47 I went out night after night through the snow to collect goats' milk from the neighbouring farms. Fortunately a well-known general surgeon in Colwyn Bay, Dr Currie, cured the defect: Morris began to put on weight, and thereafter never looked back.

The business continued to grow and to prosper, though it was hard work: in those early years I was working most of the hours of a seven-day week. The visible rewards were beginning to appear: by 1948 I had bought my first Bentley. I was eager to expand further. There was great pressure for British companies to export (but not the many practical schemes of support that there are today). We began to receive export orders from London and Birmingham confirming houses, and these made me realise the potential of the export market.

How were we to get our name known around the world? We were so small that nobody really bothered with companies our size. Then, by luck, a copy of the journal *Overseas Machinery Market* was delivered to us. It contained articles on British-made items on sale in the export market. We decided to advertise in those pages. Because of the cost, I think we arranged a Board meeting to take a decision to insert a series of advertisements over a period of 12 months. From this modest start in 1948 began an export business that was eventually to sell to 156 countries around the world.

Though export credit facilities were beyond our financial capability, and we had to insist on confirmed Letters of Credit from first-class banks, enquiries began to come in and we soon appointed our

first two overseas agents. It was tremendously exciting. We produced a simple duplicated catalogue, and flew over to Brussels to set
up our first export agency with Adrien Wilputte, who ran a successful company called Eximport. He had been lucky to survive the
war. When Belgium was under German occupation he had been
transported to Germany as a labourer. He escaped and made his
way back to Brussels, where he lived for a time in a chicken hut on
land where the present Brussels International Airport stands. For six
months he endured terrible conditions, sustained only by the food
smuggled to him at night by his lovely wife Yvonne. Having survived the experience of knowing moment by moment that if discovered he would be shot as a deserter, Adrien emerged with an
unsurpassed love of life and of good Belgian food. We have never
forgotten that he started our export business. He and Yvonne have
remained the closest of friends to me and my family ever since, and
when he retired in 1990 as Managing Director of Quinton Hazell
Remax Europe SAB we all shared a marvellous weekend in
Brussels, remembering old times.

Our second export agency soon followed. On a very happy day
in 1948 I was approached by Mr Tan Yew Kong who was interested
in taking an exclusive agency for Quinton Hazell products in
Malaya and Singapore. I flew out to Singapore, staying at the
famous Raffles Hotel, savouring the pleasure of sitting beneath the
air mats cooling the rooms, looking out at the palm trees immor-
talised by writers such as Somerset Maugham and composers like
Noel Coward.

Mr Tan Yew Kong proved to be an eminent Chinese business-
man, with a base in Kuala Lumpur and Singapore. Since the war he
had also been selling in Borneo, Sarawak, the Philippines, Indonesia
and Siam (now Thailand). It became obvious that as all the dealers
in the area were Chinese, it was essential for us to have Chinese
representation. Kong and I spent days visiting the dealers. They
looked at the catalogue, they approved the samples, but above all
they liked the box, and particularly the Dragon symbol. We had
adopted it, in a design by my brother-in-law Peter Dighton,
because of the company connection with Wales. The Chinese are
very superstitious: by purchasing a product bearing the Dragon

symbol (particularly something as vital as a steering component) their safety would be assured by the Dragon.

So Mr Tan Yew Kong became our agent. Subsequently he became Managing Director of Quinton Hazell (Far East) Limited, as he is still, in his eighties working as long and as hard as he did when our association started. For 40 years he has been first my very close associate, and then (with his family) a close friend. Throughout all these years I have found the Chinese tough when buying but excellent in paying: the Red Dragon of Quinton Hazell can be found in virtually every wholesaler in Singapore, Thailand, Malaysia, Borneo, Sarawak, Indonesia, the Philippines and Korea.

In 1950 I was driving my car on the north side of Manchester when I came to a bridge over the Bridgewater Canal at Worsley. A group of people were shouting and gesticulating, and when I stopped the car one of them asked if I could swim: none of them could. The canal beneath the bridge was in a deep gully cut through the rock: a child was in the water, and obviously near to drowning. I threw off my jacket, pulled off my shoes and dived from the bridge parapet. Fortunately I managed to get hold of the boy, who was in his last struggles. I swam with him along the canal to a point where the canal towpath made it possible for willing helpers to drag the boy and me out. After artificial respiration he regained consciousness and was taken away. Very wet and bedraggled I continued my journey: some friends lived nearby and luckily were in. They gave me a hot bath and dried me out.

Some months later I received a letter from the Council of the Royal Humane Society: I had been awarded their Certificate for Bravery in Saving Life. A ceremony was shortly afterwards held in Llandudno, where the Chairman of the Bench, Mr J.L. Simcox, made a very pleasant speech and presented the award. Wenna arranged a lunch party at the Abbey Hotel for my family.

For several years afterwards, the boy's father sent me a special Christmas cake with his grateful thanks, always bringing me up to date on his son's progress as a swimmer. This was because I had asked him, from the day after what had almost been a tragedy, that he should make sure that his son and all the children he knew would be taught to swim as soon as they could walk. Over the years, with many people having more leisure and holidays in the sun, and with great popular interest in Olympic swimming, many more people now swim. My message to parents remains the same: make sure that children can swim as soon as they can walk.

Life in North Wales was always bustling: Wenna and I had a wide circle of friends. Many of them we had known from pre-war days; others were friends I made in the army. I took an active part in local political life, and in 1950 spoke for Garner Evans, the successful Conservative candidate in that year's election.

Each morning a group of us would meet to spend a quarter of an hour in Buckley's Cafe in Colwyn Bay, which was run by Dick Moore, the former captain of Hampshire Cricket Club. We would discuss the current economic and political climate, and have serious discussions on the business situation. Among those often present were Arthur Bennison, our solicitor; Jack Rodgers, who gave me good financial advice (and often completed *The Times* crossword in a few minutes, while talking); Doug Haig, director of Braid Brothers, and my pre-war boss; Jack Judge, area manager of the Phoenix Assurance Company; and Fred Roberts, known as 'Fred the eggs', who died early from injuries sustained when he went overboard from a destroyer into the frozen sea, escorting a wartime convoy to Russia (he was in the sea for less than a minute, but the damage was done).

Arthur Bennison also died too young: he had served as a Group Captain RAF during the war on counter-espionage duties; he was a most able solicitor and police prosecutor, well respected in North Wales. He and his wife Gwen were close friends of ours; his advice in my early business career proved over the years to be invaluable, and his loss was a great shock.

In 1950 Arthur Bennison became Company Solicitor when a new Board of Quinton Hazell was formed. I was Chairman and Managing Director, with Wenna as Company Secretary. My father and brother-in-law John Holt were advisers. Arthur Millar was a great help as our Chartered Accountant; Jack Rodgers, also a brilliant accountant, was financial adviser on special projects. Bert

Matthews, who had been with me in the army, was in control of export documentation and records. Their help and guidance will always be remembered by me. I also recall from those years with gratitude, as I have good cause to do several times in this story, the help and support of Reg Plimmer, then Manager of the Midland Bank at Deganwy.

We were beginning to expand, and in 1950 bought the Ormond Supply Company Limited of Dublin (later to be Quinton Hazell (Ireland) Limited). In the search for export packing I met the Managing Director of No Nail Boxes at Chester: their product was light, strong and extremely practical for export packing. The Managing Director was Gerald Nabarro: he had just been elected Member of Parliament for Kidderminster, and a firm friendship developed between us on both a business and personal basis.

Sir Gerald Nabarro (he was knighted in 1966) became a notable figure on the British political scene. His flamboyant character added great charisma to the House of Commons: his speeches for the Conservative Party, for which he travelled the length and breadth of the country, were magnificent. He would stand, hands on hips, his huge moustache bristling with invective against his opponents. But he was much more than a theatrical figure: his greatest achievement was the passing (in 1955) of the Clean Air Act, for which Britain should be eternally grateful. He and his wife Joan had a period home in Broadway, with a library full of beautiful leather-bound books, where the Nabarros were marvellous hosts. (Some years later, when Gerald was ill, Wenna and I were proud to represent the family at the wedding of his son Jeremy in Sydney, Australia.) He had a passion for cars, and was the first man I ever knew to collect personalised number-plates: at one time he owned NAB 1 to NAB 10, on his cars and the children's mopeds. He supported my company, and always attended our company meetings.

In the early 1950s, those meetings were able to note increasing profits from Quinton Hazell Limited; these were in the region of £2,000, rising to £7,000. These may not have been large, but at least they demonstrated that the business was expanding. Each year the company grew. There was a very small cash flow, but any available cash went into new machinery and technology. The country was still recovering from the war, and rationing was only ended after the election of the Conservative government in 1951.

To keep the cash flow going, it was essential to meet delivery dates. Many were the times when we worked 24 hours a day in the machine shop and the packing department to ensure that a delivery was made before a boat sailed. Our main shipping port was Liverpool: dock strikes delayed sailings, which meant that we had to run shipments down to Southampton, London or Bristol to ensure that we got the ship manifests so that we could claim our Letters of Credit. We even carried cases to Belgium and Holland to obtain shipping space, so vital was it to meet delivery dates and cash the credits.

In those days I would set out on a sales trip, often at five o'clock in the morning, to gather in orders from motor factors throughout the British Isles. In between these home trips were overseas visits to persuade agents that they should sell Quinton Hazell components. I would bring home sample steering joints from every manufacturer in the world, open up the inside and working and measure the components, checking the male or female threads and their interchangeability with other samples in our possession.

I had a workshop at home (as I have to this day). But tests sometimes spread into the house. I experimented, together with my team, on all types of assembly. Wenna was very tolerant, and used to watch me lay out the various components on the carpet in the drawing room. But once, while experimenting with nylon cups for the internal construction, I used her pressure cooker to anneal the nylon. I was not very popular when she found out!

With the success of our sales campaign, many of the other steering joint manufacturers in England formed an association against my company. Their idea was to undercut our prices on every order, until eventually Quinton Hazell Limited would be forced by uneconomic pricing to close down. The members of this group were all very successful and high living suppliers and manufacturers. One day I was invited, together with my father (who always gave me tremendous support), to lunch with these people at the Midland Hotel in Manchester. We enjoyed a magnificent meal, with champagne, smoked salmon, and steaks. Cigars followed. Finally, as the plates were cleared, I was presented with an ultimatum by their Chairman: 'Either come into the Association, where we will see you have a share of the orders – or we bankrupt you.' I didn't answer immediately. Eventually I raised the champagne glass in my hand, looked at my father, and said: 'Gentlemen, thank you for a most stimulating lunch . . .' I was fuming inside, and my grip on the glass became ever tighter until it burst, spilling the contents over my suit and the tablecloth. Assuming great dignity, I said: 'Gentlemen, you have my answer' – and Father and I walked out. Mercifully, I had not cut myself with the glass. When we told them what had happened, my mother and Wenna were a little fearful. We had precious little capital: but my word, we had kept our pride.

Over the next four years, Quinton Hazell Limited purchased all but one company in the association. They did as they had promised, and put out quotations well below our prices. I scoured the world for orders, and where I believed the order would be given to the association, I quoted even lower prices, with no intention of delivering. However my competitors accepted: and one by one, it was they who became financially unsound. One of the companies I bought was Walt Bennett Limited. Walter was a true entrepreneur and had been a sergeant major in the Dardanelles catastrophe in World War I. He had played outstanding rugby for Sale, then a very famous team, and learnt his motor experience with Crossley Motors. He built a very successful business in Manchester, but this was gradually made very difficult by my company's expansion. Walter and I came to a far from acrimonious takeover agreement. (Fortunately, in later years, he moved to the Isle of Man where we became staunch friends.) Many of his developments were ahead of their time and ultimately helped Quinton Hazell Limited.

This challenge gave me a wonderful opportunity, because another company in the association was Anders & Kitchen Limited in Huddersfield. It was opportune because they had the most sophisticated equipment and machinery. One night at dinner, Jack Rodgers, an accountant and my adviser, put forward a scheme to buy the company from its creditors by constructing a moratorium of creditors. I had never heard of such an idea, but Jack held my hand throughout the deal. We bought the company complete with all the manufacturing machinery for 2s 6d [12.5p] in the £1 including very large losses, which could be offset against future profits. We closed down the Huddersfield factory, moving all the machinery to Colwyn Bay. Per Anders Shogren, the chairman and founder, moved away to retirement in South Africa. Other companies we purchased in this phase were Chorley Precision Engineering Limited, S. & L. Components Limited, London, and Glissan & Son of Coventry.

This was the beginning of the vast expansion of Quinton Hazell Limited. As a company, we were determined to sell to every civilised country in the world, and some that were not so civilised. I travelled extensively all over the world. Potential customers were pleased that I, the Chairman and Managing Director, had flown such distances – on my Australian visits, right round the world – to solicit their orders personally. I found personal contact the key to our export success: the result was not only a full order-book, but many lifelong friendships. At home, our workforce appreciated the value of these overseas visits, and responded magnificently to the demands placed on them when I arrived back with orders. They even gave me a plaque inscribed 'To Quinton Hazell: Super Salesman'.

In the years immediately after the war, flying could still be an exciting experience. Short trips within Europe were often made in the old wartime Dakota aircraft. Checking in at the reception desk was more leisurely, but flying times were much longer. On the flight to South Africa, we would come down to refuel in Rome, Khartoum, Nairobi, Salisbury (now Harare) and finally land in Johannesburg. On American trips, one flew from London to Shannon in Ireland where a sumptuous meal was served, ending with Gaelic coffee, and then one took off for the long flight over the Atlantic to Gander in Newfoundland, a flight often made interesting by the occasional sparks that came from the engines as carbon from the exhausts flew past the window. The next morning, on the flight to New York a delicious breakfast was served from porcelain plates, with elegant cutlery. Each trip was quite an adventure.

It was an asset to be able to travel with a catalogue and boxes as functional and well-designed as ours, instantly recognised as they were round the world from the main symbol, the Red Dragon of Wales. The design, originated by my brother-in-law, Peter Dighton, in our early days, was soon envied by the whole motor industry. (We took it as a compliment that when many years later the Japanese entered the market, they used the Quinton Hazell format and part numbering system as the basis for their catalogues.) Peter and I set out to provide a clear catalogue. We found in vehicle manufacturers' lists that many items would be identical, but charged at different prices and given a different part number according to the quality of vehicle to which they were fitted. Each of our samples was priced against works cost and we competed in the market at the competitive price. This brought down the average price of components manufactured by us, and gave us an entry via the wholesalers into the vehicle distributors' stores. This practice was banned by the motor manufacturers, but the cash incentive we offered normally won the day.

We published retail price lists with a fixed wholesale discount. In those days, retail price maintenance was allowed, and our list was usually a third cheaper than those of the vehicle manufacturers. Our business practices subsequently greatly reduced and limited the price of motor components. A further discount was offered, based on monthly turnover. This discount could be deducted from the statement, as long as the account was paid strictly in accordance with our sales terms. By this method we could check monthly accounts: those that did not claim discounts were suspect, and we would re-check their credit worthiness and perhaps cancel the account. By this means bad debts were virtually eliminated and our cash flow greatly improved. I always emphasise that a keen eye on cash flow is vital to any business. Peter Dighton, as well as being in charge of the packaging, also developed the purchase and quality control department for the raw materials. He was appointed a director in 1956.

We were making our own way. Our production programme was planned following rigorous daily and monthly checks of sales per item recorded on the Cardex system. We bought in bulk so that we paid sensible prices, our minimum orders for forgings for the steering joints were 5,000 lots: our suppliers were T.B. Wellings of Willenhall, and we were marvellously supported by their Production Director, Arthur Hughes. We made ball pins from steel bar, ground the balls on a machine designed by the Works Director Geoff Schofield and Works Manager Derek Churm. The balls were hardened in an ICI cyanide bath. The moment the forgings arrived, we would work virtually round the clock to make the finished product and sell it quickly, so that we could pay the forging company bill at the end of the following month. I spent many hours working in the hardening department, and always hated the job: but it was an essential technical requirement.

In 1954 we received an export order for 2,500 pairs of Dodge truck track rod ends – our Part No. QR6. It was the largest single order we had ever received and the excitement was intense. In association with it, we received a Letter of Credit for £5,000 Sterling, then a huge sum for us. By working 24 hours a day and all weekend, we completed the order, packed it, despatched it to Liverpool and received the Bills of Loading back from Liverpool all within 12 days. This gave the company a marvellous financial cushion and allowed us to lay out further investment in more forgings.

At this time British manufacturers were still manufacturing ball joints with an adjustable base fitted with a screwed thread and then secured by a split pin – a very expensive assembly. During the war I had noticed that the Americans, developing the throw-away society, had abandoned the screwed base and spun the base on to a cap using a substantial spring on the base plate to take up the wear automatically – they were on steel-lined joints. On an earlier visit to New York I had contacted Hub Moog of Moog Industries in St Louis, Missouri. I had known the company by name as a very substantial steering joint manufacturer in the United States. I made contact on the telephone from New York and was very surprised to be put straight through to the Chairman, Hub Moog, who suggested that I fly down to St Louis to see him. He and his wife Dorothy entertained me at their home and showed me the sights, including a visit to a real showboat moored in the Mississippi river. Hub gave me free run of his factories. I had long talks with their Technical

Department and then flew back to North Wales with the necessary drawings and details of the rolling mechanism, which Geoff Schofield adapted in a hectic 24-hour session before we began production. We were motivated by the need to succeed: I believe our product proved to be better, and certainly far cheaper to produce, than anything being offered by our competitors.

While in America I also noticed that their ball pins were made from cold forgings, similar to the head on a bolt. This gave great strength, as the grain flow was formed like an onion. On an automatic bar machine the steel was cut across the grain. We soon found a bolt manufacturer in the Midlands to do this. Tests on the new ball pin went smoothly. We swung into ever larger production: once again we were way ahead of our competitors.

Sometimes we worked 20 hours a day, seven days a week. Money was always short as sales mounted and we had to maintain bigger stocks. Depending on the nature of the business, the question of stockturn is vital. In a retail shop, stockturn can be 20 times a year; in a wholesale business carrying a large variety of lines, six times is good. In a manufacturing business, somewhere between eight and ten times per annum is usually considered more than adequate. Many businesses at start-up are persuaded to carry too many duplicated lines: remember that stock has to be increased with turnover. Duplicating stock is very expensive; whenever possible, stock the line you know best, believe in it, and sell that product. Do not just choose the cheapest, but do ensure the quality – there is no profit in returned items. Stock records are essential, and today now that computer programmes are readily available and comparatively cheap, it is relatively simple to keep stock in line. The rate of movement is vital and, of course, the computer records can trigger re-ordering. But a manual check on all orders is essential. I know of several instances where a company has held a sale to clear slow-moving lines, only to have the stock dutifully replaced by a computer-based ordering system.

Our business, in those days before computers, thrived. Despite the pressures, my enjoyment knew no bounds. I was able to break into the market with four great assets.

- First, an enormous price advantage.
- Secondly, following from that, we could offer deals to existing wholesaler members of the Society of Motor Manufacturers and Traders that were just too good for them to uphold the SMM&T agreement that members would not buy through a non-approved manufacturer: wholesalers bought stocks from us at a competitive price through the back door.
- Thirdly, budding wholesalers, newly starting up, at last had a supply source.
- Fourthly, I had made my own entry with my own products into the export markets, which were developing rapidly.

Pricing policy has always played a major role in my attitude to merchandising. Manufacturing and distribution costs are always subject to enormous on-costs, where control is out of the manufacturer's hands. To discover the start of the chain, one looks to government, both central and local, where ever-increasing costs have inevitably raised the overheads of manufacturing companies. The price of services, many of which have now been denationalised, stimulate the chain since many of them are still national monopolies, able to make additional charges for their product despite huge increases in demand – charges that are often equal to, or more than the annual rate of inflation. This has encouraged an inflationary spiral that runs through electricity, water, gas, coal, postal services and telephones. Until this is stopped and we get value for money, inflation is inescapable in our lives.

This is only the start of the inflationary spiral. 'Hidden' additional costs on business and the individual are a continuous drain on resources. The PAYE (Pay as You Earn) system, excellent though it is from a government viewpoint, puts the onus of book-keeping on companies: this is one more overhead that has steadily raised the cost of production in the UK. With the introduction of VAT (Value Added Tax), companies are again made unpaid collectors. Yet a business is not allowed a genuine error without suffering heavy fiscal punishment. There is great unfairness when HM Customs and Excise require VAT to be paid on a transaction before an invoice has been settled. Time was when true manufacturing industries

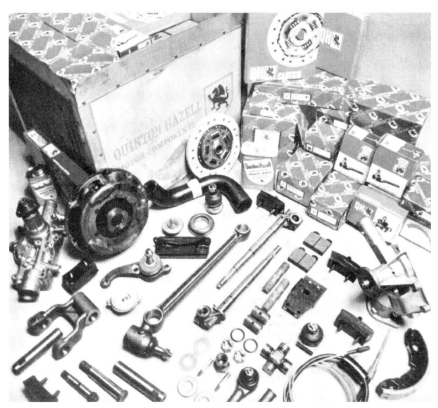

A range of our products.

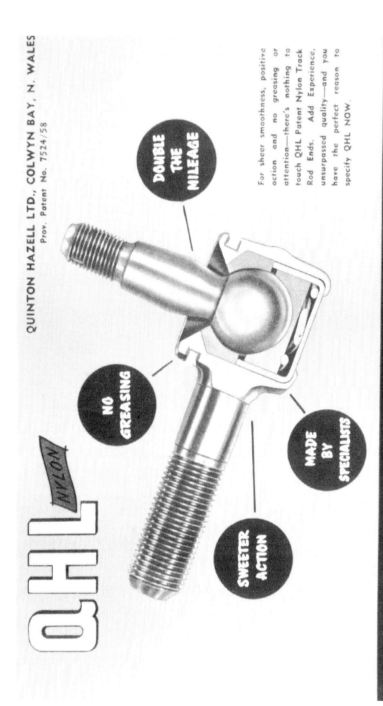

QUINTON HAZELL LTD., COLWYN BAY, N. WALES

Prov. Patent No. 7524/58

QHL NYLON

DOUBLE THE MILEAGE

NO GREASING

MADE BY SPECIALISTS

SWEETER ACTION

For sheer smoothness, positive action and no greasing or attention—there's nothing to touch QHL Patent Nylon Track Rod Ends. Add Experience, unsurpassed quality—and you have the perfect reason to specify QHL NOW.

ORIGINAL EQUIPMENT TO LEADING CAR · TRACTOR & DUMPER MANUFACTURERS

The Quinton Hazell first nylon steering joint.

IF they handed out medals for success in exporting, **Quinton Hazell**, manufacturing motor components, would collect a gold award. Approximately three-fifths of total sales is made in more than 70 overseas countries. Trading over such a wide area the company is less vulnerable to localised economic adversities. In fact, there is reason to believe profits will continue to show good expansion even though the British motor industry is in the doldrums.

Although it has Standard and David Brown as customers, the main business of Quinton Hazell is not the supply of original equipment. Instead, the group competes with the motor manufacturers in the replacement market. Furthermore, it does not restrict its activities to parts for British models, but also supplies components suitable for use in continental and American makes.

Last year, when the company's shares were introduced to the stock market, profits greatly exceeded the forecast level. To be precise, the pre-tax figure was £112,000 against an anticipated not less than £60,000. Not surprisingly a bigger than forecast dividend was declared, the payment being $22\frac{1}{2}\%$ instead of 15%. The chairman waived his right to dividend on 500,000 shares but, assuming the distribution had related to the entire issued capital, earnings cover would have been $2\frac{1}{4}$ times.

At the present price of 7s the dividend yield on the 1s ordinary shares is 3.1%, which represents a forward looking valuation. It is my belief that the necessary growth in profits to justify this and an even higher rating will be forthcoming.

Sales in the first 3 months of the current financial year were over 50% higher than in the corresponding period of 1960. A considerable order book is held for all lines manufactured by the company, and expansion of productive facilities is in progress. The floor area of the main factory at Colwyn Bay is being increased from 32,000 sq ft to more than 60,000 sq ft.

Other factories have been brought into the group through acquisitions. Glissan and Son, of Coventry, manufacturing king pins, water pumps and axle shafts, was taken over last year. Additionally, a big interest in Remax has been purchased. This concern makes and distributes electrical and mechanical replacement parts for vehicles.

Yet another expansion project provides for the setting up of a factory and distribution depot in the European market.

Finance for expansion has been found by the sale of Hutchison and Wilde, a wholly-owned subsidiary, owning and operating garages and a caravan site.

Altogether Quinton Hazell exudes the pleasing air of a small but growing company which has found a successful trading formula. Naturally, there is a little more risk attaching to investment in any rapidly developing enterprise. But in this case I think a purchaser of the shares will be able to look back with satisfaction as the years go by.

THE STOCK EXCHANGE GAZETTE 11 AUGUST 1961

Comment on the company in the financial press.

The company helicopter.

The company aircraft.

Sports day at Colwyn Bay: the train driver is Derrick Churm.

At the Colwyn Bay factory, Viscount Whitelaw in discussion with Works Director Geoff Schofield.

At the Colwyn Bay factory, Lord Snowdon appraises a silencer.

The main factory, Colwyn Bay.

Company head office, Leamington Spa.

Penhrhyd.

were charged Council rates as a half-charge. This encouraged British manufacture, and it paid to belong to the manufacturing sector. However, in later and (they say) more enlightened years, everything has been levelled up and now it is easier to import a product than to manufacture it.

Tough though life was, we were spared much of this when my business began to thrive. Our selling policy was carried through ruthlessly, moving on from steering joints to the manufacture of water pumps: here, pressure die-cast pump bodies reduced the manufacturing cost. The aluminium die-cast bodies which were a better product, requiring far less machining than the cast iron they replaced, and again reducing the price. Iron foundries were a dying business. We also made moulded impellers which were balanced in manufacture.

The company's profits increased to £18,000 in 1958, to £36,000 in 1959, and to £61,000 in 1960. The overriding problem was to see that sales did not exceed the cash flow. Certainly our products were accepted throughout the world, and we were increasing our business at home, but it was far easier to increase our sales than to increase the cash flow.

As the turnover and the number of lines we produced were increased, more and more sophistication and modern technology were essential; but this had to be sophistication without adding cost. The total production schedule was checked on large boards in the control office, which was the production heart of the business. Production schedules were always based on critical manual examination of computer records, as distortions in sales patterns could then be identified and explained: for example, a strike in a motor vehicle plant could bring us large but short-term orders for a single component.

By this time we had installed simple mechanisation for stock control: each sale was scrupulously recorded and each month the sales total for each item was listed. The great benefit of our daily, weekly and monthly sales records was that they revealed which items were increasing in popularity and which were slowing down, and should be removed from the catalogue. This saved us from producing redundant stock, though we still analysed our stock control and production schedules in minute detail as exceptional orders could distort the normal sales and production programme.

As we grew, we decided to stop recording small ancillary items singly. There were literally hundreds of small items such as nuts, washers, cotter pins, springs and finished ball pins. Large bins were introduced into the stores, with painted lines inside them giving the approximate quantities in 1,000 lots. Each day our Purchasing Director, Peter Dighton, checked the bins, noted the contents in relation to the lines, and placed orders to keep them topped up. Taking them off our stock records in this way saved many man-hours and proved so efficient that I would never advocate any other system, even in this computerised age. There were many other examples of ways in which we cut costs. For example, by introducing thread rolling machines, which speeded production by ten times the then conventional cutting method, we eliminated many tedious man-hours. Displaced staff were moved to yet further new machinery, boosting our production. Each move made us more competitive and able to sell products of higher quality.

We planned the production programme on a three-month cycle, but occasionally we would have a large order with a Letter of Credit, which meant that Geoff Schofield and his works staff had to carry on for long hours, even at the expense of modifying the main manufacturing programme. This caused enormous problems as purchases of steel and forgings, packaging and boxes were geared to our monthly cash flow. However, a large order accompanied by a Letter of Credit was our life blood, and whilst turnover was always higher at that time than it should have been in relation to our capital base, the disciplines we imposed on ourselves ensured that we met our commitments.

Later on, as the business expanded, it became clear that our methods had to be critically examined. The ratio of turnover to capital became our biggest worry: overtrading might be acceptable, but gross overtrading was certainly not. Turnover of £500,000 gave us £36,000 profit before tax. Ultimately our goal of £3/4 million turnover with £61,000 profit was achieved in 1960. At this stage, I decided that it was necessary to employ a full-time chartered accountant. Monthly balance sheets were introduced, budgetary control was fully integrated and, for the first time, we worked with a fixed budget for the year ahead and a tentative budget for the year after that. In a fluctuating market such as the motor industry it is not possible to see further ahead than these figures indicated.

We constantly updated our technology. Money was made available to us by Reg Plimmer, then Manager of the Midland Bank at Deganwy. He and the Bank supported me at every stage of our development: they trusted my judgement even when my plans may have seemed slightly over-ambitious. Reg had great vision and determination, and I owe him a great debt of gratitude. The final decision about financial support rested for many years with Carroll Jones, Regional Director of the Midland Bank, based at Cheltenham. He was the brother of Mervyn Jones, Chairman of the Wales Gas Board for many years.

A number of us worked hard in those years to try and bring new industry to Wales. In 1952 I was elected a member of the Welsh Board for Industry (North Wales). Welsh slate was the finest in the world, but working practices were very slow to change and the industry was in very rapid decline. It was essential to provide new industries to relieve the inevitable unemployment in the area. Successful factories were established in Llandudno by Coldrator Refrigeration (now Hotpoint), and in Pwllheli by a very good company, the Ceka Tool Company, now selling worldwide: a number of smaller industries sprang up through the Principality.

I considered that we were partially successful, but felt at the time (and continue to believe to this day) that a much greater effort should have been made to establish a large horticultural enterprise in the Llyn Peninsula. The Gulf Stream ensures good winters, and holiday makers appreciate the congenial climate during spring, summer and autumn. I still hope that the benefits of this lovely area will be more fully utilised.

Wenna and I loved the area we had known for so long. We had many friends, and would have dinner with them at the Imperial Hotel, run by an excellent hotelier, Eric Cox. North Wales was very beautiful, and we enjoyed our long walks by the sea on Sundays at Treaddur Bay with our West Highland terriers, and picnics in the Lledr Valley near Bettws-y-Coed, watching the salmon leap. Deganwy was a wonderful place to bring up children. Our son Morris went to day school in Colwyn Bay, and after school he spent every afternoon on the beach. Wenna's great friend was Nesta Crossley, broadcaster and writer of children's stories. Her husband, Gunga, was Head of Science at Llandudno Grammar School. They had a boy, Ceri, of the same age as Morris; they would walk on the beach and Nesta would tell them marvellous stories as they hunted in the sandhills.

Eventually we moved five miles south from Deganwy to a most beautiful house, Penrhyd Hall. This was just a mile from Lord Aberconway's Bodnant, with one of the most glorious spring gardens in Britain. We were fortunate to have a similar situation to Bodnant, benefiting from the mild climate of the Gulf Stream, with beautiful spring rhododendrons and azaleas. We were lucky to have an excellent gardener, Mr Williams, who nurtured every flower and shrub with devotion. There was a walled garden in which we grew raspberries commercially, providing one of the earliest crops in Great Britain. We also had large greenhouses where we imported azaleas from Holland and Belgium for the Christmas trade. This convinced me that a major horticultural business would prosper. But I was already working on my own business more hours than I could possibly count, and the weekends in this glorious valley were a much-valued relaxation.

Quinton Hazell Limited continued to prosper. At Mochdre we had built a new factory on an adjoining site, so deliveries of steel no longer had to be carried up 25 stairs. But the place was bursting at the seams and I was considering building a new custom-designed factory. We were also perfecting the design of the world's first successful nylon steering and suspension joints, which I was convinced would take us to still greater success. We had added to our technical team Peter Baker, a further Technical Director to support Works Director Geoff Schofield and Works Manager Derek Churm. We had set up an apprentice training school, which together with day-release classes at the Technical College in Colwyn Bay would ensure that we could continue to recruit high quality engineers locally.

Our export order book was well stocked, with all the necessary documentation efficiently handled by Bert Matthews and his team.

There were substantial orders from Singapore, Malaysia, Thailand and India. Then in the summer of 1956, when we had been in business with steadily increasing success for ten years, the blow fell. The Suez Crisis happened: the Suez Canal, our main delivery line to the Far East, was nationalised by the Egyptian Government, and blocked for a time. Shipping had to be re-routed round South Africa while the international crisis sorted itself out. I promised my workforce that there would be no redundancies; but with a rapidly expanding business, it was necessary to sell the product and be paid.

We had to do some fast thinking and planning. New markets must be found, and quickly. I made my plans, and went to see Reg Plimmer at the Midland Bank in Deganwy. I explained that I proposed to expand sales in America, increase sales in Europe, establish a new larger depot in Ireland, and take on a distributor in the South of England (Charles Thompson in Reading). I proposed, on top of that, to push extra sales into Australia and New Zealand. To achieve all this, I would need additional financing, and time to repay. Reg listened to what I had to say, and realised that he must put this to Head Office. He took the train to London. I waited at the station for his return. As soon as I saw him, I knew he had succeeded on behalf of my company. In a matter of three months, we had corrected our course. We did not lay off a single employee. Indeed, in the whole of my period as Chairman and Managing Director, we never did stand off a single member of our workforce.

In 1958 I was appointed an MBE for Service to the Export Industry. Wenna and I went to Buckingham Palace, where the award was presented by Her Majesty the Queen. Afterwards Wenna and I had luncheon at the Connaught Hotel with some of our close friends.

CHAPTER FIVE

GOING PUBLIC

By the mid-fifties Quinton Hazell Limited employed about 800 people and this virtually eliminated all unemployment in Colwyn Bay and its area. Good wages also helped the local shops, garages and other industries. Our ever-increasing sales were stimulating great jealousy from our competitors, and also from the car manufacturing giants who up till then had never had consistent policies for the sale of components. (Today, they have all copied my original idea and the vast sales organisations of Unipart, Moprod, Ford and Vauxhall emulate the lead provided by Quinton Hazell.)

Planning the next range of products, introducing sophisticated modern machinery, and balancing the cost of that machinery against the increase in efficiency, became an art. I have mentioned earlier that we had always hardened our ball pins in a cyanide bath: this was a dirty and potentially dangerous procedure and while in the early days I took my turn at it, I hated the operation. Then a new hardening machine was introduced into the market, using high frequency electricity with special high carbon steel in the component and simultaneous head and quench. The machine was a high capital cost for those days, but we worked out that the saving in manpower and the improvement in quality made it a viable proposition. After several nights of meetings and discussion, we finally purchased the machine. It soon proved its worth, giving strict quality control and very fast output, thus lowering our costs per item. We could harden to exactly the depth we required. Our product was improved, and increasing sales figures soon demonstrated the wisdom of our decision. Once again staff were moved to new production lines, as sales and production increased.

Since then, the rapid development of electronic controls has made the effective life of sophisticated machine tools much shorter. New technology means that machines must be replaced more often; certainly they are faster and more accurate than their precedessors. In the case of computers, the changeover cycle may be even faster. Depreciation policy allows a write-down on most machinery at a maximum of 20% over a straight line. By the time a machine needs replacing, with the price inflation of recent years and the additional cost of new technology, the price may have escalated by perhaps 100%. So we face a write-down on a £200,000 machine of £135,000 over five years, with a new machine costing probably £400,000: this is a straightforward deficit on capital of £265,000. It is no wonder that Britain's manufacturing industry is short of capital, yet our life blood depends on the introduction of new technology. I believe that Government should encourage industry by an additional annual allowance for depreciation, adequate to allow for inflation, to get Britain's heart beating again.

We continued to expand our export markets: an introduction from Adrien Wilputte, our Brussels agent, enabled us to start selling in Holland where Ben Staartjes, a magnificent man and great Olympic yachtsman, began to fly our flag. Then we entered the Norwegian market. Crossing the Atlantic again, I visited Toronto and Montreal for orders, after which we began shipments to Canada. In the United States, Bill Harris, head of Phoenix Assurance of America, provided me with an office in New York equipped with an invaluable set of trade directories. Then I went on to South Africa, India and Ceylon (now Sri Lanka), and finally to Australia and New Zealand.

The expansion of the business meant that we had to find more factory space. I decided to build. I have always preferred freehold property. Many pundits say that you should not tie capital up in property, but with a freehold (albeit on a mortgage) you can approximate your fixed costs. You have to buy carefully, and property sometimes becomes completely out of step with other costs (as in 1985–88). But the advantage of a freehold is that no landlords can send the rent sky-high just at a time when you need to consolidate the business. Further, freehold property with parking space can only increase in value over a given time span.

In 1956 I started negotiations with Colwyn Bay Borough Council to purchase a site which had been professionally filled and levelled by the Corporation at Mochdre, tipping having stopped there before the war. It really was a beautiful site, bordered on two sides by gently sloping hills, the south side facing down to Glan Conway and the Snowdon range. There were ten acres of flat land that had been well consolidated, but the Borough Engineer was very much against our developing the site since he believed that anything substantial built there would sink. However, if I would take the risk (and at £50 an acre who wouldn't?), I was assured that planning permission would be granted. My reply to the Borough Engineer's worries was that if the building sank, we would have the largest basement in Wales. I consulted my architect, Iscoed Williams in Penmaenmawr and additionally my very good friend Edward Jones, a master builder of the highest repute. We agreed to dig some bore holes and put in test pieces over a period of six months to measure the deflection. These tests proved eminently satisfactory and plans were drawn up for British Reinforced Concrete to prepare a huge steel raft to cover the building site. Iscoed made detailed plans, including a roadway round the factory. All the drains were pre-dug and fully finished at the same time as the raft was installed and the concrete poured.

This gave us a clear well-drained site with the road foundation and kerbs laid before we began the erection of the steel-work: this stage was therefore able to proceed on a remarkably clean site. Edward Jones and his son Ifan, with a project manager, built the whole factory in six months. The main roof had a north light, the brickwork was beautifully finished, and there was an imposing office block facing south. Oil-fired boilers heated the whole factory, there was an electrical sub-station to give all the power we required (and to serve another innovation, our first super computer). There was a gatehouse with comfortable living accommodation. The final touch was a range of flagpoles enabling us to fly the national flags of visitors from countries all round the world, together with the Union Jack and the Red Dragon of Wales.

Finally, we planned the move to take place over one weekend. Our old works in Mochdre was bulging at the seams and speed was essential. All the overhead power lines in the factory were ready in place, and by working non-stop from the Friday night after the works closed down, we moved every machine, all the stock and the offices, and began work on the Monday morning without one hour of production being lost. Everything was planned to split-second fine timing, with a fleet of low-loader vehicles, furniture vans and our own transport. Each machine had been pre-located on detailed plans by Geoff Schofield, our Works Director, and everything went without problems, except for damage to one drilling machine.

In the new factory, production was planned with a daily production target which attracted a bonus when it was achieved, each member of the works sharing in the daily bonus. Once the target was achieved, a red lamp high in the roof switched to green: every member of the workforce was dedicated to efficiency and once the light turned green, singing would start and production went into overdrive.

The workforce had a great sense of belonging. From the very start of our business, the annual Christmas Dance was a huge success. Before Christmas, the works staff were given an afternoon off for shopping, once the Club money and the Christmas Draw had been paid out. On Christmas Eve there was always a staff party in the offices, which was much enjoyed. One Saturday each summer we arranged an Open Day, with train rides, pony and trap and horse riding for the children. Athletic sports were organised for the children and the works staff: one year the marathon was won by Eddie Tan, Tan Yew Kong's son (a most popular win). The fields surrounding the new factory were landscaped with games pitches, and the Quinton Hazell Football Team showed great prowess. In the winter we organised darts matches, and on 5 November there was a fireworks party for all works members and their families and friends. On cold winter mornings, we provided hot Oxo free as the workers arrived.

My critics called it paternalism. But the factory never had a single industrial dispute whilst I was Chairman. The workforce refused to be unionised: we ran with a democratically elected Works

Committee, whose Chairman had immediate access to the Works Director. (I remembered Harry Pollitt's remarks to my father during my boyhood.) My door was always open to works personnel and their problems: I was happy to give advice, and I kept a fund from which I dispensed cash to settle problems when I believed the distress was genuine. The cash was always a gift, with the slate thereafter wiped clean: I never believed in loans. In my dealings with the workforce I was following the pattern of my life in the Garden Village, at school and in the army, creating what I have believed in all my life – the team spirit.

One of the most notable developments in the new factory in 1956 was that of the nylon-lined steering joint, which did away with the grease nipple that hitherto characterised that joint. This design was also incorporated in steering suspension joints. We conducted many thorough tests over a period of two years in many different settings: among them was a group of selected taxi cabs in Canada, and racing cars on test tracks. Finally on Saturday 15 March 1958 I set out for a long-distance road test. I drove the Jaguar Mark 7 saloon in British Racing Green, fitted with the nylon-lined steering joints (and with flagstaffs carrying the Union Jack and the Welsh Dragon, and Welsh dolls decorating the windows!) My companions were Geoff Schofield, Works Director, and Harry Gilchrist, as navigator and photographer. We were flagged away from the City Hall in Cardiff by the Lord Mayor. We knew we were proving an important new product, and the results of our tests gave us the confidence that the venture would succeed.

We drove the car some 10,000 miles through rain and slush, through snow in the Alps, to Italy and finally the South of France. At the end of each day Geoff would remove the joints from the car and examine them very critically for any sign of wear. At the end of our road test, wear was minimal. Mike Hawthorn, the famous British racing driver, showed tremendous interest in the product and was most impressed. He gave us the signal to go, and we changed over our whole production to nylon steering joints. The design is now used virtually worldwide. However, our original patent application failed on a mere technicality. A design many years earlier had shown bronze bushes to hold the ball pin and, although nylon had not been invented when this patent was granted, it was so drafted that I could not obtain a patent on the full design. We did get part of the assembly method covered, but other manufacturers could copy round this.

We made track rod ends for Colin Chapman, first for his small Lotus factory in London, and later at the Wymondham plant. Colin wanted us to make suspension joints with a nylon encapsulated ball pin and no lift in the joint at all. In a racing car, the normal steel suspension joints allowed bounce on the front wheel in cornering: the product we designed totally eliminated this clatter. When Colin won the World Championship for the first time, in 1963, he sent Quinton Hazell Limited a telegram thanking us and our suspension joints for materially contributing to his success. This was only another of the many developments in which Quinton Hazell Limited were way ahead of the conventional thinking among car manufacturers: today practically every car is fitted with nylon steering and suspension joints. Interest was aroused in other markets too: tractor companies such as David Brown saw the potential of maintenance-free steering. The replacement market, here and in exports, liked the product. We swung into record levels of production.

We decided on the standardisation of ball-pin ball diameters to $3/4"$, $7/8"$, $1"$, $1^1/8"$ and $1^1/4"$. Our machinery was designed to accommodate these sizes on individual transfer machines with only height or length having to be adjusted, a matter of perhaps ten minutes' part number changeover time, with preset tooling ready to slip into work.

Over the years we made many developments that are now universally used. These include the general use of pressure die cast aluminium water pumps with plastic and fibreglass impeller, the further development of universal clutch cover assemblies fitting a large range of vehicles, and drive couplings for the Mini which trebled the life of the component. By the end of 1958 we were exporting to 58 countries: exports accounted for 78% of our sales. We had sold more than one million track rod ends.

By this time Quinton Hazell Limited and I as its founder and Chairman were earning wider attention. I was beginning to be invited to participate in activities outside the motor industry. In 1958 I was appointed a Director of the Union Marine Assurance Company in Liverpool, a section of the Phoenix Assurance in London. This was my first major company directorship outside my own business, and I was tremendously thrilled. I had close connections with the Phoenix Assurance Company Limited as my brother-in-law John Holt was branch manager in Manchester, and my great friend Bill Harris was head of the Phoenix in New York (he was later to be Chief General Manager, and then Deputy Chairman of the Phoenix), and played a great part in helping me sell in the North American market. He had a wide circle of friends and his help was invaluable.

In 1961 I was appointed a member of the Welsh Advisory Committee for civil aviation. We met regularly under the Chairmanship of Sir Miles Thomas, formerly head of the British Overseas Airways Corporation (BOAC) and of Morris Motors. We therefore shared a mutual interest in the motor industry, and he was at all times very helpful to me. This association with civil aviation provided another link with my good friend Gerald Nabarro, since his factory was on the edge of Hawarden Airport, to the west of Chester, and the local airport for North Wales. Hawarden Airport was run by the Hawker De Havilland Aircraft Company. (Little did I know that some years later Sir Arnold Hall, as Chairman of Hawker Siddeley, would appoint me a director of that company.)

At that time, before the building of the motorways, journeys from North Wales to London were very slow. The train service took five to six hours. Gerald and I suggested to a Liverpool-based airline, Starways, that their morning flights from Speke Airport, Liverpool, could call at Hawarden, and similarly the evening return flight. After many talks with the owners of Hawarden Airport and Starways, a scheduled service was announced: it would make it possible to complete virtually a full day's work in London and return home to North Wales in the evening. The day of the inaugural flight arrived, with much publicity in the newspapers and on the radio and regional TV. We flew successfully to London, and were at work before 10 a.m. On the return flight in the evening, hardly had we taken off than we were being served free drinks, and then four boys in outlandish gear took over the centre aisle and sang to guitars in a way we had never heard before. It was a marvellous atmosphere, and really stimulating impromptu entertainment. This was my introduction to the Beatles!

A few years later I was invited by Mervyn Jones, Chairman of the Wales Gas Board, to become a board member. Mervyn's brother Carroll had helped me in financing my business when he was regional director of the Midland Bank. On Mervyn's retirement, he was succeeded by Emrys Evans, a great Welsh personality and friend of mine who is a great ambassador for Wales not only in the UK, but also in the USA. I had many trips to Cardiff in those years to discuss business and Wales in general, and rugby football in particular. From 1966 for two years I also served on the Council of Bangor University (now the University of Wales at Bangor).

In 1960, therefore, life was very rewarding. I had created and built up a successful company of international reputation of which I was proud. I was prosperous, and had a lovely home. Life in North Wales was good. My staff was happy and well regarded, and we worked as a team. We had a range of successful products. But I saw a much greater role for Quinton Hazell Limited. We had a substantial turnover and profit, but for the next stage we needed to turn the company into a vehicle with public shares, and the resources to grow by judicious takeovers. If we launched a public company, it could carry the bank loans that up to that time had been entirely my personal risk; that would enable us to make further investments in the latest technological equipment for the new factory on its ten-acre site.

It was a dangerous step from my point of view. I realised at the time that I would no longer be the owner, but be responsible to shareholders. Also, as my personal shareholding decreased as a percentage, though it would doubtless increase in value, the company might well be at risk of a takeover. There were long discussions, involving Wenna, my accountant Arthur Millar, my solicitor Arthur Bennison, Jack Rodgers my friend and accountant, and of course my team of directors, Bert Matthews, Peter Dighton and Geoff Schofield.

We decided that we must progress and become a public company.

I called on Jack Dawes, a barrister working in an issuing house, and he introduced us to an eminent chartered accountancy firm, Robson Rhodes. Its senior partner, Robert A. (Bob) Douglas, verified our accounts. It was necessary to have London solicitors considered essential by the Stock Exchange to present the offer, and in 1960 our brokers Tilling & Row floated our one shilling [5p] shares at 1/10½d [just below 10p] on profits of £60,570 (such a sum would be around £600,000 today). The launch consisted of £200,000 in 4 million ordinary shares of 1s. Some of the financial papers warned that the shares were not for widows and orphans. How wrong they proved to be: in the following year, 1961, our profits were £112,000, the dividend was increased, and dividend and bonus continued in this pattern for the next 12 years. The directors at the launch were myself as Chairman and Managing Director, Bert Matthews (Executive Director), Geoffrey Schofield (Works Director), Peter Baker (Technical Director), and Jack Dawes.

Our concentration on export sales meant a steady stream of overseas visitors to be entertained. Not all of them could make the long journey from London to Colwyn Bay, and I found that more and more of my time was being spent arranging overseas visits to meet our customers in their own countries, or entertaining them in London. Annual General Meetings of the new public company were held in Colwyn Bay, where I would each year present a resumé of the year's changes and forecast development in the year ahead. These meeting were very well attended; but I seemed to be spending a lot of time travelling to and from London, or passing through Heathrow Airport: the continually growing export market took us often abroad to new associates, as when Geoff Schofield and I flew out to India to visit the new factory built by Quinton Hazell (RANE) Limited in Madras. Most of the machinery in that factory was built at Colwyn Bay. (I was able to make a small promotional point when, on returning home, I sent a Welsh red dragon flag out to that factory by BOAC Comet, so that it could fly alongside the Union Jack opposite Madras Airport for the arrival of the Queen for a visit to India shortly afterwards.) We also began to make trade visits to Australia where in 1966 we formed Quinton Hazell Australia Pty.

The Motor Shows, then held in Earls Court, London, were a very special feature of the business and our stand was enlarged every year to accommodate the enormous number of visitors. We would invite our major agents from overseas and arrange to accommodate them in London hotels, with our directors and managers detailed to see to their entertainment in the evenings. On the final night of each Motor Show, Wenna and I would host a large dinner party at the Hyde Park Hotel, attended by a glittering array of overseas visitors and important home customers with their wives, together with distinguished guests from industry and politics.

My travelling to and from North Wales was wasting a great deal of time. We purchased a small distribution depot in Brixton, London, which had two flats associated with it. One was used by the manager, and for a time I used the other as a London office and base. Eventually we decided that we would have to relocate the office somewhere more centrally placed in Great Britain, and in the early '60s we moved our Head Office to Hazell House in Leamington Spa. With some sadness and regret, Wenna and the family left Wales and moved to live in Birdingbury, a beautiful village eight miles from the office. There are many compensations: overseas travel has become much easier, since we are now only half an hour's drive from Birmingham Airport and two hours from Heathrow and London, where we usually spend some two days a week. We have many friends and a lovely home; but sometimes I long for the Conway Valley, the view of the mountains with Snowdon at their peak, but more than anything a walk with the dogs by the sea.

The British motorway system was beginning to open up, but in the 1960s the roads were not adequate for us to provide a weekly delivery to every customer in England, Scotland, Wales and Ireland. The distances meant virtually two hours of dead mileage before we could begin to reach our customers, and the drivers were having to spend many nights away from home. So we purchased a distribution depot in Coventry, a fine building with moving tracks, high stores binning and easy selection facilities.

We purchased Remax Limited of London, distributors of motor components, and E. Steiner Limited of Birmingham, who had been automotive component suppliers for 40 years. With a fleet of 20 large up-to-date vehicles based in Coventry, we could deliver to the majority of customers and have the vehicles return within the day. As they drove back into the depot the vehicles would pass through an automatic wash before refuelling, so that the fleet was kept gleaming fresh. Larger trucker vehicles made daily trips from Colwyn Bay to Coventry to keep the depot stocked. Export sales packaging and despatch remained in Colwyn Bay.

Scotland proved difficult for our deliveries. There were no nationwide carriers then, as there are today. Our next plan therefore was gradually to establish wholesale depots throughout the country. These supplied local garages and additionally, by the orderly marketing of our products and strict adherence to a discount policy, we were able to supply the local factors who would compete on equal terms. I must confess that there were important centres where other component manufacturers used bullying tactics and would refuse to supply a customer if they stocked Quinton Hazell products. Heavy hands require heavy action. We found that if we set up a warehouse almost next door to such people, the bullying soon ceased.

To strengthen our distribution in Scotland we purchased Alexander Cheyne Limited, a public company and highly respected as a distributor of vehicle parts and cycles, based in Aberdeen with established branches in Glasgow and Dundee. We could then make bulk shipments to Glasgow and Aberdeen and split them among other distribution points. To Alexander Cheyne we soon after added Ajax Precision Engineers, Kerry's (Great Britain) Limited, the Edmund Fox Group covering Carlisle and the Borders, Shortis of Norwich, and the Johnson, Burton & Theobald Group of Norwich. Together these became the Partco Division of wholesalers within Quinton Hazell plc.

Our distribution in Northern Ireland was run by Stuart Knox, a former employee, who built his own highly successful business (now being run by his sons and daughters, and still going from strength to strength). In Ireland we had, in 1950, purchased a small distribution company, Ormond Supply, which was owned by a larger-than-life Irishman, John McGrotty. As we were a Welsh company with a close affinity to the Southern Irish, and a good sea connection from

Holyhead to Dublin, we were able to guarantee swift and punctual deliveries. In 1953 larger premises were bought in Dublin that enabled us to do some assembly there, and thereafter our products became highly competitive in the Irish market. Now in the 1960s this business was further enlarged.

The next development was in the replacement silencer market. With the great increase in the number of motor vehicles, together with the steadily rising speeds of which they were capable, it became obvious that there was going to be great potential in this market. Cars were using petrol of higher octane rating, and although the quality of silencers was constantly improving, they were having to cope with ever increasing heat through the system. We knew of a successful silencer and exhaust pipe business (A. & Z. Silencers Limited) in Lytham St Annes, Lancashire. They employed modern techniques, making quality silencers with double wrapped outer skins with seamed ends which were superior and yet much cheaper to produce than welded end plates. They also produced great numbers of exhaust pipes, and finally manufactured a most sophisticated exhaust clamp: they named it 'Banelli' from the own-ers' names (Mr and Mrs Bancroft were a husband and wife team). We bought the business as the basis of Quinton Hazell Silencer Division, based in Lytham. We manufactured and sold hundreds of thousands of Banelli silencers round the world; today they continue to be used universally. We subsequently purchased A.G. Buchanan Silencers from Sandy Buchanan in Birmingham, and Ce-Last Silencers from the Bolton Gate Company.

Economies of scale directed us to amalgamate these businesses, and so we bought a huge new facility at Warton Airfield just out-side Lytham. The fabulous but ill-fated TSR2 aircraft had been manufactured here, but its cancellation meant that part of this fine factory became available. There we made a huge replacement range of exhaust pipes and boxes covering British, Continental and Japanese motor manufacturers' models. The corporate title of this part of our operation became Quinton Hazell Silencer Division. Bert Matthews moved from Colwyn Bay to Lytham to be Managing Director. We adopted the best processes from each com-pany, bought the latest technology in pipe benders and automatic presses, and through our own toolroom (headed by a superb engineer) introduced even more sophisticated machine developments. Eventually the products moved along an unbroken production line, ending up in an automatic electrostatic spray booth, after which the parts were numbered and then sent to stock and despatch. Later it became clear that we should develop silencer and tyre fitting shops, which we did under the name of Standard Tyre and Exhaust Centres.

The logic of this development, the manufacture of the complete exhaust system and the sale, not only through the very large factor chain which we serviced, but through our many Exhaust and Tyre Centres was again a first in the United Kingdom. Sales through our fitting stations generated cash, and from raw steel to fitting and cash in the bank could be as quick as five days.

I feel I must pay tribute to Tommy Farmer CBE who has developed a magnificent business in Kwik-Fit plc, and shown the great potential that knowledgeable and specialised fitting can produce.

The exhaust pipe business also took us into South Africa. I was on a sales trip there in 1963, and staying at the Edward Hotel in Durban. Two South African businessmen, Herby Jacobson and Jack Levi, who manufactured exhaust pipes in Johannesburg, heard I was in the country and, unknown to me, came to Durban and booked into my hotel. Then they contacted me with a proposal that they should represent us in South Africa. Over two days of discussions we agreed that we would form a joint company, Quinton Hazell Superite. Some time later I discovered that the moment the ink was dry on our agreement they paid their bill and hightailed it back to Johannesburg, as at that time they could not afford to stay in Durban one day longer. My years of association with Herby and Jack and their design director Neville Cohen were highly successful and very pleasant. Neville was a man of great intellect and ability, coupled with a fortitude that enabled him despite his handicaps to compete in the Paraplegic Olympic Games. The company we set up had enlightened views on management and employee relationships, and proved profitable to all parties.

At this time I also developed a components business in Australia and New Zealand, buying premises in Enfield, Sydney, to distribute our products in Australia. The deal was completed for me by our Australian Managing Director and his wife, Trevor and Marie Hutchins, who are still personal friends: after retiring from our company they later developed a successful import business dealing with Japan and Korea. From our early beginnings in Sydney we developed a manufacturing facility there, and then a silencer (muffler) facility in Melbourne. Machinery made to our specification was manufactured in the United Kingdom and shipped to Australia: business steadily expanded, and I was particularly pleased when our son Morris (who had served an apprenticeship at Colwyn Bay) travelled out to Sydney to help develop the company. We then followed the plan we had introduced with Partco in the UK, buying a chain of wholesalers beginning with F.H. Gardiner Pty in Sydney, and expanding into Brisbane and Adelaide with further distribution in Melbourne.

The Australian supply and replacement market was dominated by Repco, who controlled manufacture and distribution of components through the Wholesalers' and Spare Parts Association (WASPA) which was a group with exclusive power similar to that of the Society of Motor Manufacturers and Traders (SMM&T) in pre-war and immediate post-war Britain. In the first years of our operation in Australia there was a constant fight as wholesalers were threatened with losing their entire list of franchises if they dared to stock Quinton Hazell Australia components. However, our quality and terms were good. Our own wholesale chain sold into the market, the garages were content with our pricing policy, and gradually as we developed in Perth, Northern Territories and Queensland it was evident that we were winning and the stranglehold was loosened. Throughout my life I have believed that if you have a just cause, and are prepared to batter on doors day after day, week after week, even the stiffest opposition eventually weakens and fails. It gives one a great glow of satisfaction to succeed.

Meanwhile in Britain our own fleet of vehicles now delivered throughout the country on the same day at the same time every week. We employed a battery of telephone girls who contacted the customer 24 hours before the vehicle started, to check whether any extra items were required. This was in addition to our field sales team. It is sometimes said that salesmen should be paid solely on results, with a low basic wage: for any greater reward he has to fight all the way. I disagree completely with this principle. A salesman has to be contented, and keep his head high. He should be provided with a motor vehicle that reflects his status in the company. His basic salary should be enough to ensure that he can plan the purchase of a house and have a regular holiday with his family: how can he keep the dignity and respect of his customers if he cannot leap that first hurdle? However, so long as the company has given adequate training, a salesman who does not perform should be dismissed: sales are the lifeblood of a company. In my company, salesmen's commission in one year was added to their basic salary for the next, with the commission base starting at the previous year's sales achievement. We thus had contented, well paid and loyal staff who had the opportunity to progress to greater responsibility as area Sales Managers, Sales Managers and even Sales Directors.

We attracted good staff, not least because we were recognised as being aware of the latest technologies. In 1968 we bought Kelly Ultrasonics, a leader in ultrasonics design and manufacture, and also the Morris Rubber Company, which was developing rubber to metal bonding technology: these formed the basis of our Specialised Companies Division. Quinton Hazell Limited was now highly structured in communications. The company was growing very quickly. We purchased a helicopter which was based in Leamington Spa and soon proved its worth. We could visit Colwyn Bay, and Lytham, and throw in a trip to Carlisle and be back at head office the same day. Our directors could keep a keen eye on the development of each section of the business. Spencer Kendal, a veteran helicopter pilot of the Malaysian War looked after us.

Eventually the growth of the company in Europe, and particularly our increasing links with France where our friends were distributing our products from a large warehouse in Orleans, made an overwhelming case for the purchase of a twin-engined aircraft with the capability of flying easily to these countries, as well as to Italy and Denmark. We found a very good aircraft and a first class pilot, Captain Peter Jones, who flew a regular European round robin journey and also made regular visits to our various subsidiaries. It was a bonus, for example, to fly to Aberdeen, land with supplies of parts, visit customers and then return with a cargo of fresh lobsters and other delicious seafood. The aircraft was also available to ferry customers to our factories: this proved to be a first-rate public relations exercise, since the customers could see the goods being produced, and note the care, technical ability and emphasis on quality exercised in our factories.

The plane had six seats, and my secretary Janet Glover used to accompany me with her typewriter so that on the return journey I could dictate to her, and she could type a record of the day's events. Janet did a thousand and one jobs over this busy period, arranging world travel, conferences, and appointments, and generally running my office. My excellent personal aide at this time was Charles Rowsell, a chartered accountant who joined us from De Havilland at Chester. A first class administrator, as a Director of the company he looked after my welfare, watched my back and steered me away from pitfalls. When he retired, I missed him to my continued regret.

We had developed an enormous range of components. Most of them (apart from our introduction of nylon suspension and steering joints) had not been changed in principle by the motor industry for 40 years. For example, an exhaust assembly consisted of a front pipe, one or two silencers, and a tail pipe. The configuration of where they were located varied with the design of each model of car. To make the assembly fit, it was necessary to follow or copy the route employed by the car manufacturers. By sophisticated tooling, and using spun ends on double skin casing, we greatly improved the quality and speed of production.

There was a similar situation in relation to clutch assemblies. The production bolt-on covers were designed to coincide with long-established clutch assembly configurations: the positions of the fitting bolts were standard except on diameter, and assemblies could be made to fit not only British, but in many instances also French, Italian, German and Japanese applications. Our critics said that it was an impossible task to tool up for a full range of covers and plates to encompass the world – but we did.

One might suppose that a nation concerned with earning from exports, a nation importing more and more motor vehicles from overseas, would be pleased that a British manufacturer was prepared to make such components for the motor industry, saving vast sums of foreign currency meanwhile. Not so. The Copyright Design Act 1971 was so widely drawn by Parliament that virtually every item could attract copyright protection. The slightest bend in a silencer pipe, or divergent shape of a clutch cover, could be copyrighted; the penalties for breaching copyrights were enormous, even if the original patents had expired long before. The vehicle manufacturers saw their replacement spares base being eroded, and sought to use this Act to put component manufacturers such as ourselves out of business. It was a short-sighted policy on their part, since years later most of them copied the Quinton Hazell distribution system and introduced multi-make supply.

For us, this legislation was a great worry, particularly in relation to clutches. I was attacked for copying a clutch cover assembly. A long series of meetings ensued. Eventually we agreed to purchase a number of clutches from Automotive Products through our subsidiary Partco. Meanwhile we were permitted to sell our existing stocks, but would change the design of our product. This was a challenge, but our design team immediately faced the problem of making an alteration. We redesigned the outer shape, so that while the depth and bolt holes coincided, the outer appearance was subtly changed.

Then we set to work on the interior of the clutch, testing the resistance of the diaphragm spring on every clutch for every vehicle, and plotting a graph of pressures. It quickly became apparent that on a small pressure difference, clutches fitting up to 20 different vehicles were virtually the same. If we went to the highest pressure, there were perhaps 2 lbs between the highest and lowest. The pedal pressure felt the same and reacted perfectly, but clutches with 20 part numbers could be covered with one reference. I think eventually we worked out that only ten different clutch assemblies could satisfy 150 applications. What a boon that proved to the wholesalers, and what a disappointment to vehicle manufacturers and their suppliers. What a success for Quinton Hazell Limited: the clutches fitted vehicles made all over the world, greatly increased our exports, and reduced specialised imports into Britain. We called the clutch range 'Q 10000'. It has been a best seller for over 20 years. Where there's a will, there's a way: repressive legislation in all spheres is sooner or later beaten (as the nations of Eastern Europe and the former Soviet Union have shown).

But it was a long and tough battle. Harry Hooper CBE, Chairman of Armstrong Equipment plc, fought an expensive action in the courts over a bend in a silencer pipe, and I attended court as an expert witness. Other firms were challenged over body panels. The lunacy was running right through British industry. (I brought the unfairness of this legislation into the open in a long article in the *Sunday Times* in 1970; many companies and individuals suffered until a sensible amendment to the Act was finally introduced in 1988.) Once competition is eliminated, one sees prices spiral. Taken to a conclusion, such legislation could have driven the price of ordinary household items such as 13-amp plugs into the stratosphere. If one seeks proof of the effect of true competition, consider long distance bus fares in a business that is highly competitive, compared with British Rail which has no direct competition on its lines – as yet.

In 1968 (having been a Director of one of their subsidiaries for ten years) I was elected to the main board of the Phoenix Assurance Company Limited of London (I was to serve as a Director until the company was taken over by the Sun Alliance Assurance plc in 1984). The monthly Board Meetings were very interesting, as we had presentations by the various divisional heads on the risks taken in relation to air transport, shipping, burglary, fire and life policies. Our Chairman in the early years was Lord De L'Isle VC KG PC: with my friend Bill Harris (of New York) he guided me through my early meetings. Other companions on the Board included Field Marshal Earl Alexander of Tunis KG PC, a charming man who was my hero from wartime days, Sir William Dugdale, head of the great Warwickshire family, and Sir Robert Mark, once head of the Metropolitan Police: I had known Robert since his Manchester boyhood, when he played county-level lacrosse with my brother

Maurice. Also on the Board in my time were Sir Arthur Bryan, Chairman of Wedgwood Limited, a master potter in his own right and sometime Lord Lieutenant of Staffordshire; Jocelyn Hambro, City banker and later Chairman of Phoenix Assurance; Hugh Astor, a great aviator among other accomplishments; Lord Adeane, former Private Secretary to the Queen; Sir Seymour Egerton, Chairman of Coutts Bank, to be followed by David Money Coutts; Sir Arnold Hall, Chairman of Hawker Siddeley, the scientist who identified the fault in the Comet aircraft, and subsequently helped to develop the Hawker Jump-Jet aircraft; and Patrick Crichton, Deputy Chairman of the Foreign and Colonial Investment Trust.

The conversation at meetings of these people was remarkable, and I was greatly honoured to listen to and take part in discussions with men who had helped to shape our nation. I believe I was responsible for the Phoenix plotting on its computer the age of car and motorcycle drivers, and identifying the proportion of accidents involving young drivers. This led to a more cautious approach to insuring the young, since it made clear that safe driving improved with age. The evidence showed that drivers of 17–21 were the worst risk, those of 22–25 rather better, and from then the risk lessened with age. Today older drivers receive much more advantageous insurance premiums.

Patrick Crichton introduced me to the Board of the Foreign and Colonial Investment Trust, the oldest and most respected of investment trusts, where I met another group of remarkable people: Sir Nicholas Henderson, sometime Ambassador to Washington and Paris; Sir John Egan, of Leyland and then Jaguar; Derrick Baer, former Chairman of the Foreign & Colonial Investment Trust; Hugo Baring, of the distinguished banking family; John Sclater, Chairman of the Foreign & Colonial Investment Trust, and of S. & W. Berrisford; and Lord Nicholas Gordon Lennox, former Ambassador to Spain. At our monthly meetings we listened to a luncheon guest, each of them at the top of British industry or government, who would brief us on his speciality.

(Later I was appointed founder Chairman of the Foreign and Colonial Enterprise Trust which specialised in injecting capital into new companies that we believed showed promise. This was a fascinating job: the leg-work was done by James Nelson, grandson of Lord Nelson of Stafford, and Andrew Barker, a former Oxford rugger blue, who specialised in the American market. It was a fascinating period and FACET, as it is now known, is a well-established public company in its own right.)

In 1971 I was asked to visit the then Secretary of State for the Environment, the Right Hon. Peter Walker. He asked me whether I would be prepared to be Chairman of the West Midlands Economic Planning Council. The retiring Chairman was Sir Adrian Cadbury: the challenge that he put to me in a series of talks was so stimulating that, despite my very busy industrial schedule, I accepted the appointment and threw myself wholeheartedly into the office. It happened that the Prime Minister, the Right Hon. Edward Heath, was in Birmingham on the day I was inaugurated into the job.

The monthly meetings consisted of detailed discussions with industrialists, academics and trade union leaders: I valued the excellent advice given by high calibre civil servants. I learnt a great deal about the working of government in those years, and had the pleasure of meeting and dining with senior ministers. I was impressed that the West Midlands Economic Planning Council, despite its wide range of members, tackled each problem with great thoroughness, and never with rancour.

My appearances on radio and television became ever more frequent; there was some straight talking about the many problems that manufacturers faced in a region that was then the powerhouse of Britain: in those days there were many more individual manufacturers, and Birmingham was rightly called the City of a Thousand Trades. But infamous legislation by the Labour Government from 1964–70 caused the demolition of some major factories and the removal of roofs to avoid paying rates. This led to the diminution of British manufacturing, which reduced employment of the working population from almost 50% in the 1960s to 35% in the 1990s. How can one manufacturer support two service industries on his shoulders? I saw, in my time on the Planning Council, the best of British workmen led by some thinking union leaders who could see how industrial relations must change in the late twentieth century.

But their jobs still, at that time, depended on some of the more militant leaders in the factories: 'Red Robbo' was among the best known in the Birmingham motor industry, and Jack Dash in the London docks. The dock union attitudes had already virtually destroyed the prosperity of Liverpool and London docks.

The year 1969 seemed to be likely to lead to still greater prosperity for Quinton Hazell Limited, but for me that spring brought an event of great sadness. My dear father, Tom Hazell, had been a key to any success I had achieved. I have written earlier about the invaluable support he gave me in my boyhood in Burnage, in the foundation of my company, and at each of the crises that are bound to arise in business life. He was a superlative craftsman: he was also personally brave. I am told that during the war, when his beloved timber works in Salford was ablaze from bombing, he fastened a mattress on top of his car and drove through the blitz to help fight the fire. After the war, we were real pals: his advice was always available to me, and always sound. Then early in 1969 he suffered a heart attack, and died on 6 April. I was with him just before he died, willing with all the strength in my body that he, my greatest friend, would live: but to no avail. In the years that followed, whenever I had to make a big decision I thought what Father would do in such circumstances: he never failed me. I think of him every day, and will always love him.

My mother survived him for five years. She lived in Rhos-on-Sea with her sister, my Aunt Dolly. She loved life and was full of fun; her passion was bridge which she played every other day, and would discuss her hand for the whole of the next day. She had a small car, and enjoyed a good hotel luncheon, and afternoon tea in the country. Her life was dedicated to her three children; she was greatly proud of all of us, and kept a scrapbook to record everything we did; because I was reported more in the papers, there was much about me, since she managed to track down any newspaper in which I figured. She loved to attend factory functions and presentations in Colwyn Bay, and was always kind and thoughtful. Suddenly in January 1974 without any warning she was stricken with leukemia. She was rushed to hospital, but did not long survive.

At least my mother was able to share with us our pleasure at the marriage in 1970 of our son Morris to Tricia Barton, at Stoneleigh Church. Her mother and brother own a long-established antiques, furniture and glass business in Leamington Spa. She is pretty, intelligent and full of life. Our much-loved granddaughter, Lara, was born in 1972 at Claverdon, Warwickshire, and our grandson, Morris, in 1975 at their home in the Isle of Man.

Wenna and I were also delighted to be invited by the Earl Marshal to attend the Investiture of HRH Prince Charles as Prince of Wales at Caernarfon Castle in July 1969. The day was perfect and in good time our Rolls Royce headed out across Conway Bridge, through Penmaenmawr, Llanfairfechan and Bangor and on to Caernarfon. Our seats were within 50 yards of the dais; I felt proud to be at the ceremony, and will always be able to picture the pageantry, the flags, the colourful uniforms, and the splendour of Her Majesty the Queen performing the crowning ceremony, with the youthful Prince replying in the Welsh language. For Wenna and myself, and our workforce at Colwyn Bay, our presence on that occasion was a fitting celebration of more than twenty years of fruitful and productive service to Wales and to Britain.

CHAPTER SIX

TAKEOVER

When in 1971 we celebrated the 25th anniversary of the company, we looked back to those early days just after the war when four of us set up a motor-car components shop. Now, a quarter of a century later, we could share with our four thousand employees the satisfaction of belonging to a highly successful enterprise trading round the world. The previous eleven years, from the time when Quinton Hazell Limited went public, had been particularly vigorous and expansive, concentrating as we did upon self-dependence. The company was now so dominant that machine tool specialists could design and build original Quinton Hazell equipment and plant that was far cheaper and very much more efficient than anything the company could have bought in the market.

Well-established and much-respected companies in the motor spares trade became merged into the Group by means of a policy of production and service prompted by a desire to provide the best products for the widest possible markets. The increasing number of items manufactured and stocked meant that our catalogues and publicity had to be clear and logical, epitomised in our CERT coding which placed each component into its appropriate group: C for Cooling, E for Exhaust, R for Rod Ends (Steering and Suspension) and T for Transmission. Each of these catalogues was more than a list of items: the catalogues were clearly planned, well laid-out systems for customers to use with the minimum of effort in the hectic day-to-day turnover of urgently needed vital components.

Our central headquarters, Hazell House in Leamington Spa (a traditional country house, bought five years earlier and subsequently enlarged), was conveniently close to the Home Sales Warehouse in Coventry, and also accessible to all parts of the country through the growing motorway system.

The year 1972 was one of continued progress. A new extension was added to the Colwyn Bay factory. At Redditch, Worcestershire, a factory was acquired from the Birmingham Small Arms Company Limited, where the Transmission Division could be put together under one roof, incorporating a number of other companies we had acquired: W.H. Briscoe & Company Limited, brake and clutch drive plate manufacturers from Tyseley, Birmingham; Aero & General Machinists Limited from Walsall, and Colray Engineering Company Limited from Tamworth, shortly afterwards followed by Lea-Francis Engineering from Balsall Common. Meanwhile the Sales Administration was being brought together at the Balsall Common, housing the entire CERT Home and Export Sales, and the Retail Division.

In 1972 Quinton Hazell Limited was awarded the Queen's Award for Industry, for Export Achievement. This much prized award was inaugurated by HM The Queen to recognise outstanding year by year percentage increase in exports, and also technical innovation, leading to a sustained increase in Britain's export performance.

From the company's foundation Quinton Hazell Limited had concentrated on directing a substantial proportion of its turnover to the export market. From our earliest years I had personally embarked on many export missions to all parts of the world, in days when overseas travel was still not easy or comfortable. Nor were the trading conditions: those were the days of Empire Preference, and of trading blocks such as the East African Federation: but when the Mau Mau troubles erupted in Kenya, the East African Police required motor vehicle components to maintain their highly efficient peace-keeping force mobile: we supplied tens of thousands of pounds of components to this force.

Wenna accompanied me on many of those long-haul trips and hosted receptions in many countries. The Empire, often much maligned, kept law and order and ensured trading relations. I believe our journeys to Australia were our greatest pleasure in those years, but we travelled to many of the 151 countries to which, by that time, we were shipping motor components. Even at times of recession, when one country's economy declined, another would open up: the scope of our export markets was literally for us a world sales insurance policy.

The Queen's Award was presented to Quinton Hazell Limited at a large reception on the works playing field at Colwyn Bay by Colonel Sir Watkin Williams-Wynn as the Queen's representative: it was a moving moment for me, since he had been my commanding officer at the outbreak of war. Afterwards he had been transferred to a regiment at Singapore, where he was captured by the Japanese. Following the presentation ceremony, the assembled company proceeded to a celebration lunch at the Maenan Abbey Hotel in the Conway Valley. It was a very happy and gratifying occasion.

By 1973 Quinton Hazell Limited had 104 Partco branches in England, and several in Holland, with a joint distribution company (Quinton Hazell Netherlands), and also a joint distribution company in Belgium (Quinton Hazell Remax). In South Africa there was Quinton Hazell Superite Pty Limited; in Singapore, Quinton Hazell Far East; and there was Quinton Hazell Australia. Quinton Hazell Ireland virtually controlled the Southern Irish market, while Stuart Knox and his company distributed in Northern Ireland. In Scotland, Partco branches were run as a distinct Scottish Division.

We were also developing Standard Tyre and Exhaust Centres with Merritts Tyre and Exhaust Centres, and had plans to expand these by providing customer waiting rooms with free coffee, discount offers, and an associated brake and clutch fitting service. This was all on the drawing board when, in 1973, Quinton Hazell Limited and all its subsidiaries were taken over by the Burmah Oil Group. The price paid was £56,000,000.

Over a period of 27 years Quinton Hazell Limited had virtually changed the face of British motor component manufacturers and distributors. We were manufacturing in a diverse range of factories, employing always under one thousand people on each site: this made it possible for our blend of management by works committee to operate fairly and effectively. I believe that we had developed a

Presentation of the Queen's Award for Industry by Sir Watkin Williams-Wynn.
On left, Eric Pemberton, Managing Director of the Colwyn Bay factory.

Congratulations to

MR QUINTON HAZELL M.Sc.

OUR SUPER SALESMAN.

ON THE OCCASION OF THE PRESENTATION OF

"The Queen's Award to Industry"

FROM ALL WORKERS & MANAGEMENT QUINTON HAZELL LTD. COLWYN BAY
28th JUNE 1972

Congratulations from the works on the Queen's Award.

To : E Quinton Hazell Esq, M B E
Chairman
QUINTON HAZELL (HOLDINGS) LIMITED

From : Works Committee Members
Quinton Hazell Limited
Colwyn Bay

6th April, 1971.

Sir,

On behalf of all the personnel in the Production, Assembly, Casing and Packing Departments here at Colwyn Bay, it gives us very great pleasure on this very special occasion to express our gratitude and thanks for giving us the opportunity of being employed by your Company, which has experienced no industrial disputes whatsoever over the past 25 years.

The happy atmosphere that we are enjoying at the Colwyn Bay factory is second to none, and for this we feel much credit is due to the management for making us feel we are just one big, happy family.

There is an Industrial Relations Bill going through Parliament at the moment - Sir, as you are already aware, we have enjoyed good industrial relations at Quinton Hazell Limited, Colwyn Bay, for the past 25 years. May the success of the Company continue in the future.

We cannot let this occasion pass without thanking Mrs Hazell for the role she has played in making the name QUINTON HAZELL world-wide known and respected as it is today.

We all say together, MANY THANKS!

WORKS COMMITTEE REPRESENTATIVES
1970/71

A 'thank you' from the works committee.

The author with the cup presented to him personally on the completion of the acquisition of the Lea-Francis car company.

The Earl of Denbigh and HRH Princess Margaret with the author.

Meeting the Rt. Hon. Edward Heath, then Prime Minister, in Birmingham.

At Buckingham Palace for the presentation of the CBE.

The opening of the new wing at Warwickshire Private Hospital 1989. Left to right: Mike Tansey (Chairman), Sir Dudley Smith DL MP, the Mayor of Warwick, Dame Jill Knight MP, the author.

The Board of the Supra Group. Left to right: Stephen Neal, Richard Neal, the author, Peter Dighton, Jack Dawes.

My son Morris and his wife Tricia.

My grandchildren Lara and Morris Adam.

With Wenna at my seventieth birthday party, December 1990.

manufacturing and sales position unequalled in the United Kingdom, and spreading throughout the world. Our policy was consistently to sell the best product at the best possible price.

My own control of the company had been eroded as my personal capital base was small and acquisitions — many for shares, which were taken by either the target company owners or by the marketplace through the stockbrokers James Capel, as they were an eagerly sought-after share — reduced my own holding to about 6 per cent of the company. I believed, wrongly, that my fertile ideas would protect the company from takeover. Unfortunately, this was not so and with such a knock-out offer as £56 million I could not blame the shareholders who took enormous capital gains on accepting the Burmah paper, regarding it as a very successful takeover.

At the takeover I was elected to the Burmah Board as a non-executive director. I believed I was going to be given the Board's backing to develop Quinton Hazell Limited, with the greater financial muscle of a large group. There was still so much to do. I believed that my entrepreneurial skills could be used to develop Halfords and Rawlplug, which were within the Burmah Group. Theirs was a situation I understood completely: my plan was that Halfords would distribute Quinton Hazell products through their retail chain, which had shops on every high street. I was aware that Halfords were contemplating the launch of exhaust and tyre centres. We were manufacturing silencers in Lytham St Annes, and through Standard Tyre had 100 distribution depots throughout the country fitting tyres and silencers. These, I thought, could complement the proposed new centres, giving us ever better margins. Our centres could be tied in with Halfords as customers, again giving constant and positive cash flow. (It is interesting to see that Halfords have greatly enlarged this service.) Rawlplug distribution would be widened through Halfords and Partco, and through the huge overseas connections of Quinton Hazell Limited and Burmah's Castrol Oil. Finally, the topping-up of these outlets could be handled through the nearest Partco depot of Quinton Hazell.

When I put these ideas forward to the Burmah executives, I was told to my face by Nicky Wood, the Burmah Group Chief Executive (a solicitor by training), that it was questionable whether I was capable of running my own business (for which Burmah had just paid £56 million), and that I was not expected to put "foolish suggestions" forward. I had already been instructed that Quinton Hazell would thenceforward sell only Castrol oil and brake fluids. Our outlets had previously sold our own high quality Quinton Hazell oil and brake fluids, using them as door-opener sales products since both were substantially cheaper than the Castrol product. I had thought the addition of Castrol to our sales would be an added bonus.

I was then told by my new colleagues to produce a forward budget projection of sales and profits over the next five years, with details of exact components to sales. This is impossible in the motor industry, and quite pointless when one considers the changing pattern of vehicles and countries of origin. In fact, in 1972 most cars in the United Kingdom were made in Britain; by 1976 the flood of foreign imports had begun.

Over a period of weeks I lost every argument, and with such evident lack of confidence in my judgement there was no point in staying in such an environment, and I had no option but to retire. It was the hardest decision I have ever made in my life. I had lived, dreamt, slept and eaten the motor trade in every fibre of my being, and had built up a prototype of how I believed the industry should be run. Quinton Hazell Limited was the acknowledged leader in its business throughout Europe. Now, at the age of 52, I was obliged to retire. All the years of apprenticeship, the planning during the war, and the 27 years of stewardship of an increasingly successful company were devastated and lost to me. This was a very sad end to a most eventful era as far as I was concerned. But there is no future in living in the past: life always provides another challenge.

Over the years, as Quinton Hazell Limited faltered under its new direction, I tried to buy it back, but could not get any response. Later I tried to purchase an interest in the company, but the die was cast and the business was sold in separate sections. Quinton Hazell Automotive Engineering is now owned by an American company, the Echlin Corporation, run by Fred Mancheski, operating in the United Kingdom and on the Continent of Europe. Quinton Hazell

Standard Tyre was sold to Bosal (Holland), together with the silencer factories. Partco became a management buy-out: now once again this major component distributor has reasserted itself, led by Peter Redfearn, a former director of Quinton Hazell Limited: Partco has also bought out GKN Autoparts.

But the idea of vertical integration, essential to the motor components industry, was scrapped. I am certain that there is still time to rebuild the concept – it was ideal. Now the vehicle manufacturers have copied the pattern I introduced, and operate a similar system through their distributors. Today's formula of buying products in from Germany, Italy, Japan and Korea breaks the mould, and I believe offers a poor substitute. Distribution warehouses through which manufacturers' profits are taken overseas are no match for the home produced component. Britain must be a manufacturing nation, and the UK will surely return to the Quinton Hazell plan one day.

My retirement was of course personally distressing. I was loyally supported by Wenna, my family, and my many friends round the world. It was a reassurance to be able to relax in the gardens of our beautiful homes at Birdingbury in Warwickshire, and at Eze-sur-Mer in the South of France. At Eze-sur-Mer our neighbour and friend is the Dowager Marchioness of Huntly, who reminds me of my wartime army experience in the mountain training regiment at Huntly in Aberdeenshire! Other good friends there include the owners of the fairytale hotel Cap Estel, Robert and Carmen Squarciafichi.

In Britain, Wenna and I have gained great solace, companionship and pleasure over the years from our dogs. I have mentioned the walks we enjoyed in North Wales with our West Highland terriers, Pippa and Penny. In 1963 to complement them we adopted our first Alsatian: Dolly was given to us by the police after a burglary at our home. She was a beautiful girl: we lost her in 1975, she is buried in our garden, and we will always remember her. She was followed by Dolly II, who died in 1988. Now we have Dolly III, a perfect lady with a guide dog pedigree, who loves Katie, our present West Highland terrier. You learn so much from dogs. They never complain. They are true friends who, if you talk to them, understand a very large vocabulary. They always welcome you home – although when we return from a holiday or trip abroad, Katie virtually ignores us for the first hour, showing her independence of spirit.

It was the greatest pleasure to us to keep in touch with a large number of friends round the world, to visit them from time to time and have them stay with us in Birdingbury. Among those many dear friends I recall Gerald Nabarro (who died too young, in 1972) and his family, Adrien and Yvonne Wilputte from Brussels, Hub and Dorothy Moog from St Louis, Missouri (Hub, a real gentleman and friend, died in 1988), and Tan Yew Kong and his wife Lynn from Singapore. We have had the great joy of staying with them many times, and enjoying their boundless hospitality. We had the pleasure of helping to educate some of Kong's children in the United Kingdom: Eddie (the marathon runner!) at our factories in Colwyn Bay and Lytham, George on many visits, and Philip who took articles with Bob Douglas of Robson Rhodes in Manchester and is now a partner in Price Waterhouse in the Far East. Kong's daughter Lynne is now a hospital matron in Melbourne, Australia. We are proud to be Auntie Wenna and Uncle Quinton to the family. Tan Yew Kong had a distinguished war record, fighting the Japanese in the jungles of Malaya. He is now Vice-President of the Malaya and Singapore Ex-servicemen's Association, of which Prince Philip is Patron. Kong accompanied the Queen on her visit to the Far East, still contributes time and energy to war charities associated with the Duke of Edinburgh and the Prince of Wales, and is still, in his early 80s, the very active Managing Director of Quinton Hazell (Far East) Limited.

Towards the end of 1973 I decided that I must get back to work, and find another public vehicle to develop a range of products, that would be in most respects, but not totally, different from the Quinton Hazell ranges. I spoke to David Rowe-Ham, senior partner of Smith Keen, Cutler in Birmingham (later to be Sir David, and Lord Mayor of London). Within a few weeks, he offered the prospect of my taking a large shareholding in, and developing, a public company in the Midlands, Supra Chemicals & Paints plc.

Supra Chemicals & Paints, founded by Philip Neal and now run by his son Richard, was a superb company. They were large manufacturers of sound deadening sheet and pads and supplied virtually all the car manufacturers with their requirements, and the tractor cab manufacturers also, together with specialist acoustic applications throughout the British and Scandinavian markets. The company also manufactured an excellent range of paints, emulsions, floor paints and underbody paint for the vehicle industry. Supra Chemicals & Paints were extremely progressive and employed a large technical staff with modern laboratory facilities to ensure that they were at the leading edge of the business.

With myself as Chairman of the Group, over a short period we began to develop it. In 1979 we purchased a superb office complex: Marble House, Warwick. This building bristled with history. It was here that we prepared catalogues, ran the company accounts and performed the Head Office administration. I invited Jack Dawes, who had originally floated Quinton Hazell Limited and was a director in my original company, and also Peter Dighton who had been a Managing Director with Quinton Hazell Limited to join the Board. It was an unenviable task to expand a totally new concept on to the old established business, with a Board majority that was effectively the old company. It was a real challenge to increase overall profitability speedily, and to enlarge the business while attaining the agreed profit criteria.

We bought a small distributor of motor components, John Wilkinson Limited in Southam, Warwickshire. John had worked for me in Quinton Hazell days as a specialised buyer, and had used his experience to assemble a good line of brake disc pads from Italy: he had a very special relationship with Franco Pulucci and his team in Ivrea, near Turin, whose company, Gomet, made rubber drive couplings and joints. I was particularly pleased to meet Franco Pulucci and his wife Jose, since it took me back 40 years to the time when as a boy from Manchester Grammar School I had camped with a school party in the beautiful Aosta Valley.

New premises were purchased for Supra in Southam, Warwickshire. A computer system was installed to control stock, book-keeping and accounts, and the range of products was gradually increased. Having invented the nylon steering joint with my previous team, I thought it obvious that we must include it in our progamme. We began to manufacture steering and suspension joints in a factory we purchased in Colwyn Bay. We found running a small works with a relatively small staff was very inefficient, and so we took a big decision to move the total production to Supra Pressings in Cradley Heath. This move delayed our production of steering joints, but we now had another range to add to our list, and sales grew very quickly.

There was another pleasant personal occasion to celebrate when in 1974 I was appointed CBE, and once again presented with the insignia by Her Majesty the Queen at Buckingham Palace. Once more we enjoyed a family luncheon at the Connaught Hotel.

At this time I made several visits to the Gomet company in Italy. The management team was excellent and knowledgeable; the quality of their products was superb, but the factory premises were hopelessly out of date and ill-equipped. There were debates in the Supra Boardroom about introducing enough capital to pay off the debts, and to buy a green-field site for a new factory at Azeglio, near Ivrea. Since we were convinced of the quality of the management we bought a $66^2/_3\%$ stake in the business and introduced fresh capital.

Thereafter the business of Gomet prospered. In the early years, Supra Automotive provided a ready-made market for the entire rubber production. Gradually, it became clear that on the export markets, two profits were not possible. When at the start Gomet had made rubber boots for rack and pinion, steering gears and constant velocity joints, the company had seized what was virtually a virgin market. Gradually, some other manufacturers produced universal boots, and yet others made runs for the popular models. We were convinced that we had made the correct decision in deciding to manufacture tailor-made sets of boots for motor vehicles. The agreement was that Supra Automotive would distribute the product in the United Kingdom and Eire, while Gomet tackled the rest of the export market. Franco Pulucci did a superb job and very soon we were increasing production and the size of the factory yet again.

Franco quickly mastered the English language and became a first class world salesman, with Jose his wife very competently running the office and staff to great effect.

When I started Supra Automotive, it was my deliberate decision to base the majority of its products on items that Quinton Hazell Limited did not specialise in. These rubber items were our first major projects on our own, and from these were developed rubber drive joints, rubber constant velocity (CV) joints, and fan belts. Other major projects included disc pads, brake shoes, hydraulic hoses, and wheel bearing kits, including all necessary spares (the latter kits a new development on the market, and a real first for Supra). We purchased a small accessory company, Letco, in Leighton Buzzard, Bedfordshire, specialising in auto accessories, including small kits of essential items such as nuts and bolts, and we manufactured a range of special tools for the motor trade.

Except in its earliest days when we were willing to tackle almost any engineering challenge, and that included refurbishing dynamos and starters immediately after the war, Quinton Hazell Limited had never been in the electrical market. Now Supra purchased two companies in the electrical sector. One manufactured a range of sparking plug leads, made to be suitable for all engines, but with a special high tension insulation that made them excellent for electronic ignition systems. This company was Sureparts, based in Luton, Bedfordshire. The second Sureparts company we bought specialised in the manufacture of distributors, contact sets and rotor arms. This factory at Burton Latimer, near Kettering in Northamptonshire, was expanded to incorporate the plug lead business, and we introduced many technical innovations.

Back at Supra Automotive in Southam, Warwickshire, we added a division to sell, on behalf of Supra Chemicals and Paints, a range of their sound deadening pads, underseal and various speciality chemicals and garage floor paint. So taking the product package altogether, it was a vastly different range of products from those of the original Quinton Hazell business though, of course, complementary.

We developed a first-class sales organisation, covering the whole of England and Wales: we then approached Scotland by purchasing the majority of shares in a Scottish company, D. & M. Frictions of

Glasgow, whose Managing Director was George Weir. I arranged for my old colleague and friend Stuart Knox to distribute for us in Northern Ireland, and appointed a new stockist in Eire, Brian Fanning of Serfac Ltd. We provided in-house training courses for salesmen, with special incentive schemes: this ensured a happy and prosperous sales team. We added an annual sales convention and teach-in, sometimes held in exotic locations such as Tunisia, Majorca or Jersey. To these we invited some of our most important customers: this welded our team together, and the company continued to expand. Vigorous attention to the export markets was always a major plank in my business philosophy. Once again I set out on my sales travels overseas, with our Sales Director, Bert Fowler. Soon the motor trade in North Africa, Cyprus, Greece, Scandinavia, Singapore, Australia and many other countries were purchasing Supra Automotive products. I did not forget the need for distinctive packaging: Supra components were well packaged in containers with a British lion as emblem.

We directed worldwide orders to the appropriate parts of the company and its associated companies: export orders for rubber products were forwarded direct to Gomet in Italy. Our specialised lines such as wheel bearing kits, electrical lines, and once again steering joints, soon provided us with a steady and profitable world market. In this way, and in a relatively short period, Supra Automotive became a major manufacturing and distribution company, backed at all times with the cash resources and dominant position of Supra Chemicals and Paints in the sound deadening business: they supplied all the major manufacturers in the UK with their products, and some in Scandinavia.

To expand the company by buying additional specialised units, moving to the most suitable factory locations, preparing catalogues and cross-reference listings, at the same time computerising the whole system, was a mammoth task, but the team responded at all levels. Our catalogue department entered all data on computer and was most advanced in the industry, introducing new standards of information and presentation that were soon adopted by other manufacturers.

In 1985, in my 65th year, I retired as Chairman of Supra Group

PLC, and was pleased to be elected President until the company was taken over by the Evode Group plc in 1987. The story does not end here. Evode eventually sold Supra Automotive to Moprod in Birmingham, and further evolution occurred when Moprod–Supra sold to Quinton Hazell Limited in 1989.

So the wheel turned full circle.

CHAPTER SEVEN

TO THE FUTURE

———————

My life remains one of activity and interest. For example, I continue to be a Governor of the Lord Leycester Hospital in Warwick. This wonderful old foundation was created by Robert Dudley, Earl of Leicester, and licensed in 1571. The former Guildhall and associated buildings, together with St James's Chapel over the West Gate, were given by the bailiff and burgesses of Warwick to house the foundation 'for the finding, sustentation, and relief of poor, needy, impotent men, and especially of such as shall be hereafter wounded, maimed or hurt in the wars in the service of her Majesty, her heirs or successors'. Twelve 'poor brethren' are housed there, being natives of Warwickshire and Gloucestershire, appointed by the Governors from those who have suffered disability during service with the armed forces.

In 1971 Lord De L'Isle, Patron of the Hospital (whom I knew as Chairman of the Phoenix Assurance Company, of which I was a Director) asked me if I could devise a scheme to bring financial stability to this wonderful old institution. (Lord De L'Isle was the head of the linked families of Dudley and Sidney). The hospital had suffered financial problems through the centuries, from the day when the widow of its founder tried to claim it as private funds, and was only deterred when the great Lord Burghley in 1597 sponsored a further Act of Parliament to establish its legal titles. In 1971 with Charles Rowsell, my personal assistant and co-director, I discussed at length how funds could be secured, and devised an association to support the Hospital, the members of the association becoming Deputy Patrons. The association would be limited to a total of 60 families from Warwickshire, each signing a substantial five-year covenant. This has been successful, and its popularity can be gauged from the length of the perpetual waiting-list for membership. We hold two excellent social functions each year, and Deputy Patrons have the satisfaction of knowing that they are contributing to and participating in saving our national heritage. In 1986, HM Queen Elizabeth the Queen Mother graced us with her presence, visiting the Hospital and signing the Distinguished Visitors' Book, to mark the 400th anniversary of the death of the gallant Sir Philip Sidney at the Battle of Zutphen.

I was also Chairman of the Appeal Committee for a project now known as the Warwickshire Private Hospital. This was envisaged in 1979 by Mr Mike Tansey the orthopaedic surgeon, with several of his colleagues. Mrs Georgina Turriff approached me to take over the responsibility for fund-raising. The concept was to create a Charitable Hospital without shareholdings, all profits being ploughed back into new buildings and equipment. Today, the capital value is something approaching £10 million. There are 44 bedroom suites, two operating theatres, a day case unit, two X-ray machines, ultrasound, laser equipment, and a magnificent pathology laboratory.

The hospital is superbly equipped to look after the people of Warwickshire. Seeing this hospital become established has been a wonderful experience for me: for the past ten years I have enjoyed being Deputy Chairman under Mike Tansey's Chairmanship, and hope I can carry on for many more years.

From 1980 to 1991 I was Chairman of the Governors of Arnold Lodge School in Leamington Spa, a boarding and day preparatory school for some 350 boys and girls, with a most enviable scholarship record.

In 1980 I was appointed a Deputy Lieutenant of the County of Warwickshire by the late Lord Lieutenant Sir Charles Smith-Ryland.

In business, my own company, E. Quinton Hazell Limited, is the hub of the various consultancies that I take on. The past few years have been a very busy time, with the problems that the recession has caused to business. I am also able through my company to continue my interest in engineering management and supervision, and it is surprising that never a day goes by without some problem coming across my desk. A problem shared is a problem halved and many cases have been successfully completed.

I have been asked to advise businesses on many occasions. In 1985 Banro Industries plc, quality manufacturers of pressed and welding components for the motor, caravan and domestic cooker industries, was the subject of a takeover bid from Mr Tim Hearley of CH Industries plc. The Chairman of Banro, Mr Ted Rose (whom I knew well) asked me for advice and help in rejecting the bid. We had several hectic weeks of fencing and finally retained the company's independence. I was invited to the company's Annual General Meeting, at which Ted Rose very kindly complimented me on my help and then (without asking me or getting my agreement) announced that I was to join his Board. However, I did enjoy my time on the Banro Board: we had promised our shareholders a profitable future, and had to justify our promises.

Luckily this was accomplished until suddenly Ted was struck mortally ill. He asked me to sell the business, which I did, to Wagon Industries plc. My negotiations with that company through its first-rate Chief Executive John Hudson were of the highest order. Sadly, just days after the deal was completed, Ted's health finally failed and he sank into a deep sleep, never to recover. I remain a consultant to that company to this day.

In 1986 I was invited by John Davis, Chief Executive of Aerospace Engineering plc, to their Head Office in Swindon. This is a medium sized public company and its products range through aerospace components for the major aircraft manufacturers in England, France and the United States, with factories at Sutton Coldfield, Birkenhead, Worcester and Swindon. The main aircraft component factory is at Birkenhead and this factory is superbly equipped with the latest computerised machinery. Sutton Coldfield specialises in the manufacture of protype printed circuit boards. You can imagine my pleasure at being asked to chair this very exciting company and I thoroughly enjoyed my association with them.

In 1989 I was suddenly taken seriously ill, but we are fortunate in having very good friends in the medical profession; and on the immediate advice of Dr Roy Sullivan, our local practitioner in Kenilworth, Wenna spoke to our very good friend Dr Leonard Roodyn of Wimpole Street. He soon assessed the seriousness of my condition and arranged for an immediate appointment with Mr John Castro the leading urologist, and within a few hours I was in the operating theatre of the Princess Grace Hospital in London. I can only say thank you to those who saved my life at that time, and I am so grateful to be able to say now that my six-monthly regular 'MOTs' are over, and that to all intents and purposes I am as fit as ever.

Appointed to the Board of Foreign & Colonial Investment Trust plc in 1978, I continued my Board membership with a superb team until 1990. Throughout my years with the company, Mike Hart was Managing Director, handling billions of pounds. He was always considerate and completely professional. Being a member of the F. & C. Board gave me a remarkable insight into the Investment Trust industry. Unfortunately, through Board rules I had to retire on my 70th birthday in 1990.

Sir Arnold Hall formally invited me to join the Board of Hawker Siddeley plc in 1978. Sir Peter Baxendell took over as Chairman in 1989. Over the years my colleagues included my Lords Shawcross and Benson; Sir Roland Wright, former Chairman of ICI; Sir James Hamilton, former Director of the Royal Aircraft Establishment Farnborough and member of the Cabinet Office; Sir Lindsay Alexander, former Chairman of Lloyds Bank; Sir John Lidbury, and many other great men. Every Board meeting was an experience. We had regular meetings over dinner with many famous personalities, but one who stands out in my memory was Sir Frank Whittle, inventor of the jet engine and the man who changed the course of the second world war and subsequently that of the whole of air travel. In 1991 Hawker Siddeley was the target of a takeover bid from BTR that proved successful.

My years with Hawker Siddeley were very satisfying: the wide range of engineering expertise gave me enormous pride and attracted my total dedication. I had the great pleasure of visiting some of the company's factories overseas, particularly in Australia and

France. On the home front, I was particularly close to Bob Hampson, Chairman of Brush Electrical at Loughborough, and John Richardson who ran our huge battery division, manufacturing vehicle, passenger car and large industrial batteries for the rail networks, fork lift trucks and similar operations. Batteries were sold under the names of Oldham and Tungsten – companies that had helped me in the early years of my business development. My other particular interest was Lister-Petter Diesel Engines. Here, very exciting developments had just been completed when the takeover occurred.

I was particularly sad because at the AGM of Hawker Siddeley in 1991 a special resolution had been agreed by the shareholders extending my contract by three years beyond the normal retirement date. In the end, it was all to no avail.

On the political front, I have since 1984 been Chairman of the Warwick and Leamington Conservative Patrons' Club, based on exactly the same premise as the scheme I devised to support the Lord Leycester Hospital some 14 years previously. The scheme has been taken up as an example for other Conservative Party Constituency Patrons' Schemes. In 1990 I was honoured to be appointed President of the Constituency. For over 20 years in Leamington Spa I have enjoyed a close relationship with our Member of Parliament, Sir Dudley Smith DL MP.

In November 1990 I led a party to Strasbourg for a four-day teach-in at the European Parliament to try to understand more about the European Community. I returned convinced of the need for close monetary integration, but could not see how political integration could be achieved.

My family continues to be the sustaining base of my life. My son Morris, his wife Tricia and their two children live happily in the Isle of Man. Our granddaughter Lara is an accomplished horse-woman and competes with great success in equestrian events. Morris Adam, our grandson, is still at Peel School, where he is having good success on the sports field and – to his grandfather's particular delight – has played rugby for the Isle of Man schools against the Welsh schoolboys. His examination results have been highly satisfactory, and in due course he will enter university: his ambition is to be an international lawyer.

Wenna and I greatly enjoy our visits to the Isle of Man to see the family. We also make visits to our home in the South of France, and to our friends in Singapore and Australia: we still have business interests and relatives in Melbourne. These visits give us little time for relaxation, but overall I retain my full interest in business.

So here we are in 1992: a long way down the road, but still enjoying every mile of the journey.

EPILOGUE

This is my story: but as I write this, in 1992, we are still far too dependent on overseas supplies. The future, not only for the component industry but Great Britain in general, will I believe be settled when Britain decides to manufacture a greater range of products once again. In a competitive world there will be no room for large scale warehousing of imported components. Formerly, we were the envy of all nations and British quality and inventive genius spread our goods throughout the world.

We must compete with the world in technology and excellence of manufacture: to do this requires greater fiscal encouragement for true manufacture. I believe that there are many reasons why we have fallen behind, and have attempted in the course of my writing to suggest ways in which industry can be encouraged.

British motor manufacturers restrict their product guarantee to their branded parts fitted by their distributors. This policy has now been followed by many overseas manufacturers, despite the unnecessary restriction of free trade and choice. As a consequence a colossal import bill follows, which is being fostered by governments that allow such restrictions to be imposed. Regrettably, with the change of policy that seems to have been introduced by manufacturers in the UK, many components for foreign cars are now imported, and the manufacturer only acts as a distributor. In the medium term this will have a dire effect, as you cannot compete by warehousing imported components, particularly once the Common

Market has free interchange across borders. So today we see big advertisements for genuine German or Japanese parts, and the motorist is gullible and pays, say, £35 for a track rod end, where an identical part made in Britain should cost him about £8. 'Use German batteries!' shouts the advertisement: yet Britain leads the field in battery technology, and there is a British made battery suitable for every imported vehicle.

The future for our industry will, I believe, be secure when the original pattern laid out by Quinton Hazell Limited returns. In a competitive world, there will be no room for warehousing imported components, and the orderly marketing achieved by Partco and Standard Tyre, under the Quinton Hazell banner, with direct supplies from the manufacturer, was the cheapest and most effective way to combat the motor vehicle manufacturer, and the flood of cars imported from overseas.

We have the example. Motor vehicle manufacturers have followed the original Quinton Hazell concept with their multi-parts programmes; they have their own tied distributors and yet, on the replacement side, the industry has allowed itself to be fragmented. Let us make the components for replacement on German, French, Italian and Japanese vehicles. Fly the flag of one of our great British manufacturers and start telling the world once more that British components are best and are certainly competitive in a world market. Follow the pursuit of excellence through exports based on a strong home market dominance.

To encourage our manufacturing base, government must look at its policy for the manufacturer. To compete with the world, we must have the latest machinery, computer control, electronic inspection systems. This means enormous capital outlay; and this money must be spent. To enable us to do this, additional depreciation on manufacturing machinery must be allowed against tax. There is no profit in paying huge numbers of people to remain unemployed, so we must gear up manufacturing industry and make the products that Britain and the world require, which at the moment Britain so largely imports.

Why should we be importing tyres – after all, we invented the pneumatic tyre? The same applies to cycle components, including wheels, chains and pedals. Why do we import so many white goods, such as refrigerators and washing machines? We have the ability, we manufacture the compressors and electric motors. Why do we not compete? Why must we import so much clothing and so many shoes? Are our distribution systems too greedy, and do they mark up too high on our own products?

We must gear up manufacturing industry and manufacture products that Britain and the world require.

I think I have shown throughout my book that my aim was to carry the British flag throughout the world. I set out, in my area of the motor industry, to manufacture components suitable for all vehicles manufactured in the world. These components were of the highest quality, selling at a competitive price. I believe that my incursion into the parts market made those parts competitive. If similar action had been taken by other manufacturers in their fields of endeavour, assisted by a true understanding by governments of manufacturing companies demonstrated by all fiscal means at their disposal, our manufacturing base as a country would be very much larger today.

I believe there is still time to grasp the nettle of manufacturing. For too many years, buying in very cheap markets overseas has been a profitable exercise for importers, but a disaster for the British nation. I am sure that manufacturing is the way ahead, and my story has tried to show that manufacturing can be rewarding. Come on Britain – we can make it.

INDEX